Preparing Yourself for
the Vocation of Catechetical Leader

JOE PAPROCKI, DMIN

THE EFFECTIVE CATECHETICAL LEADER

Series Editor Joe Paprocki, DMin

LOYOLA PRESS.
A JESUIT MINISTRY

3441 N. Ashland Avenue
Chicago, Illinois 60657
(800) 621-1008
www.loyolapress.com



Cover art credit: Ann Triling/Hemera/Thinkstock.

ISBN-13: 978-0-8294-4524-4
ISBN-10: 0-8294-4524-2
Library of Congress Control Number: 2017936850

Printed in the United States of America.
17 18 19 20 21 22 23 24 25 26 27 Versa 10 9 8 7 6 5 4 3 2 1

# Contents

# Welcome to The Effective Catechetical Leader Series

**The Effective Catechetical Leader** series provides skills, strategies, and approaches to ensure success for leaders of parish faith-formation programs. It will benefit anyone working with catechists, including Directors of Religious Education, pastors, diocesan directors, and catechetical training programs. Combining theory and practice, this series will

- provide practical instruction and printable resources;
- define the role of the catechetical leader and offer specific and practical strategies for leading, collaborating, and delegating;
- offer approaches for leading and catechizing in a more evangelizing way; and
- describe best practices for recruiting, training, and forming catechists; developing a vision for faith formation; forming an advisory board; planning and calendaring; networking with colleagues; selecting quality catechetical resources; handling the administrative aspects of the ministry; and identifying various groups to be catechized and approaches that meet the unique needs of those various groups.

Whether you are starting out as a catechetical leader or have been serving as one for many years, **The Effective Catechetical Leader** series will help you use every aspect of this ministry to proclaim the gospel and invite people to discipleship.

# About This Book

This book in **The Effective Catechetical Leader** series focuses on the person who is *Called by Name* to be a leader of catechists. In this ministry, you are not a functionary. You are a disciple of Christ, coordinating your faith community's efforts to form other disciples of Christ. Before you focus on what you need to *know* and what you need to *do*, this book will help you focus on who you need to *be* as a parish catechetical leader.

# 1

# It All Begins with Jesus: The Call to Discipleship

It's probably a good bet that when you were a child, you did *not* dream of growing up to become a parish catechetical leader! Perhaps you dreamed of going into medicine, practicing law, taking up a trade, becoming a teacher, working in sales or marketing, or being a stay-at-home parent. And maybe you followed that dream for some time. But God had a different plan for you. When you were a child, you probably couldn't even pronounce the word *catechetical.* And yet, here you are—a parish catechetical leader.

How on earth did that happen?

## An Unexpected Calling

The faith journey that brought you to this moment no doubt contained some twists and turns. God has a way of guiding us down roads we never even knew existed. Somewhere on your journey of faith, God called you to travel down the road that led you to serve his people—the church—as a parish catechetical leader.

The first thing you need to know as you enter this privileged and splendid ministry of catechetical leadership is that you have been called by God. Too often, when we think of being called by God, we imagine a voice from the sky commanding us to undertake a specific task, much as God called Abraham and Sarah, Moses, Isaiah, Jeremiah, and Mary the Mother of Jesus. Chances are, however, there was no burning bush, no lightning and thunder, and no mighty wind accompanying your call to catechetical ministry. Most likely, you were not blinded by a divine light as Paul was on the road to Damascus. In Scripture and in human experience, God seems to prefer to call people in less dramatic fashion and typically relies on others to help issue the invitation. Your call to catechetical leadership may have come through a catechetical leader, a pastor, a diocesan leader, a deacon or religious, a catechist, or a friend. Maybe it came through an announcement in your parish's weekly bulletin or in a diocesan newsletter. However it came to you, God's unseen hand was at work. He was beckoning you into a deeper relationship with him and the church—and, after much discernment, you said yes.

## How Does God Call People?

The short answer to the question *How does God call people?* is: in a variety of ways! Take a moment to look up the following stories of God calling people, and jot down a few words that describe each experience.

| | |
|---|---|
| Moses (Exod. 3) | |
| Samuel (1 Sam. 3) | |
| Isaiah (Isa. 6) | |
| Jeremiah (Jer. 1) | |
| Elijah (1 Kgs. 19) | |
| Mary (Luke 1) | |
| Paul (Acts 9) | |

## What Exactly Have I Been Called To?

When I was serving as a catechetical leader in the Archdiocese of Chicago, both of my kids were in grade school. I recall one day going through my fourth-grade daughter Amy's folder and discovering an invitation for parents to come and speak to the students on career day. The deadline for signing up was rapidly approaching. I asked Amy why she hadn't shown me the invitation sooner. She shrugged. I asked whether she would like me to attend and speak. "No, that's okay," she responded. When I asked her why, her reply startled me: "Because I don't even know what you do."

I don't think Amy is alone. Many people have no clue what a catechetical leader is or does. And yet, according to the *National Directory for Catechesis*, "The single most critical factor in an effective parish catechetical program is the leadership of a professionally trained parish catechetical leader." Simply put, a catechetical leader is a baptized Catholic who is called upon to coordinate and animate every aspect of a parish community's faith-formation efforts, from the cradle to the grave. Simply put but not simply done! To be a catechetical leader is to be an instigator of a global movement at the local level—a movement whose goal is nothing less than the transformation of the world. In some developing countries where the Catholic Church is seen as a threat to the existing governing power, catechetical leaders are considered by the rulers to be the most dangerous individuals in the village because of their ability to inspire people with the radically countercultural and subversive ideas of Jesus Christ.

While becoming a catechetical leader has probably not put your life in danger, the fact remains that you are now in a position of great influence, promoting in your community the very same radically countercultural and subversive precepts of Jesus Christ in hopes of transforming the world one neighborhood at a time. And how do you go about spreading these earthshaking ideas? By organizing a movement.

While role descriptions for catechetical leaders vary from parish to parish and from diocese to diocese, here is a general overview of the role, excerpted from the *National Certification Standards for Lay Ecclesial Ministers*, published by the Alliance for the Certification of Ecclesial Ministry (and approved by the United States Conference of Catholic Bishops Commission on Certification and Accreditation):

> By baptism every Christian is called to proclaim the Good News. The Spirit singles out individuals and invites them to the specialized role of catechetical leader within their faith community, and many respond in faith to that invitation. As competent catechetical leaders, they collaborate with others in creating a culture of formation within their faith communities that enables each committed Christian to nurture and grow in relationship with God. As such, the catechetical leader will be well formed in the study of catechesis—its theology, its history, and its right praxis. A parish catechetical leader will:
>
> - Direct the parish catechetical program through design, implementation, and evaluation of parish catechetical processes.
> - Implement the catechumenate model as inspiration for catechesis in age-appropriate ways.
> - Develop a comprehensive lifelong vision and plan for parish catechesis based on ecclesial catechetical documents.
> - Insure the centrality of catechesis in the development of the parish as an evangelizing and catechizing community.
> - Develop and implement parish catechetical policies in accord with (arch)diocesan policies and guidelines.
> - Provide orientation and in-servicing of catechetical committee members and formation teams in their areas of responsibility.

- Exercise effective supervision of catechetical employees and volunteers while fostering leadership abilities.

Notice that this role description charges the catechetical leader with "creating a culture of formation" in his or her faith community. This is the noble task you have signed on for. But what exactly does it mean to create a culture? It means to foster conditions that lead to shared values, beliefs, attitudes, and actions among a group of people. It means creating the conditions that make people say, "That's how we do things around here" or "That's how we roll." It can be compared to creating a "climate," just as botanists do in greenhouses to foster the growth of plant life. For the catechetical leader, the task at hand is to create a culture—a climate—that fosters growth in discipleship, a life that is characterized by hunger for the mind of Christ.

## Who Is This Jesus You Are Promoting (and How Well Do You Know Him)?

Before God called you to catechetical leadership, he called you to discipleship. Through your baptism, whether as an infant or as an adult, God called you into relationship with him. God adopted you as his child, and through his Son, Jesus Christ, and the Holy Spirit, has invited you to share in his divine life. For many of us, however, the realization that we are truly sharing in the divine life does not occur at baptism. Instead, it comes through a later awakening, when our ears are opened to God's call to discipleship and we intentionally respond to that call.

For some, this awakening to discipleship happens in adolescence. For others, it happens during the college years or in young adulthood. Some experience it when they enter marriage and begin raising a family. Others experience it because of a significant event, whether joyful or tragic—the death of a loved one, the birth of a child, the diagnosis of a serious condition, a new job or a loss of a job, or a move to a new place to live. The awakening can happen in an instant, or it can happen in subtle stages over a long time. Perhaps you are experiencing this awakening right now as you venture more deeply into your role as a catechetical leader.

The bottom line is, your calling to live as a disciple of Jesus precedes and supersedes your calling as a catechetical leader. You can't give what you don't have, and ultimately, as a catechetical leader, you are being called to give to others what you have received in your relationship with Jesus—namely, a share in the divine life.

### Reflect on Your Intentionality

The degree of a person's intentionality (conscious decision) to follow Jesus varies over time. Take a moment to reflect on your own degree of intentionality in following Christ during each life stage you have experienced. Doing so can help you assess where you stand with the Lord right now and what steps you need to take to deepen your discipleship as a catechetical leader. (1 = Not Intentional; 5 = Very Intentional)

| | | | | | |
|---|---|---|---|---|---|
| Childhood (elementary age) | 1 | 2 | 3 | 4 | 5 |
| Adolescence (high school) | 1 | 2 | 3 | 4 | 5 |
| College age | 1 | 2 | 3 | 4 | 5 |
| Young adulthood | 1 | 2 | 3 | 4 | 5 |
| Middle age | 1 | 2 | 3 | 4 | 5 |
| Senior years | 1 | 2 | 3 | 4 | 5 |

Where do you stand with the Lord at this point in your life? Pray for the guidance to discern the next steps you need to take to deepen your discipleship in your role as a catechetical leader.

## In Need of a Savior

To be a follower of Jesus means to have a very clear notion of who Jesus is. In teaching about Jesus, Bishop Robert Barron reminds us of the importance of recognizing Jesus as our Savior. He explains that, today, more than ever, there is a temptation to reduce Jesus to a good teacher, a wise philosopher, a holy man who is our friend. While all of those are true, the uniqueness of Jesus lies in his identity as the Son of God, our Savior. Bishop Barron explains that if we happened to find ourselves sinking in quicksand, the last thing we would need would be a teacher or a philosopher to chat with about our predicament. We would want someone to save us!

Because of our human condition, we are prone to sink in the "quicksand" of sin and are in need of an intervention—someone to save us. Jesus Christ is that Savior. And as a catechetical leader, you have been called to remind everyone within earshot that we are hampered by sin and desperately need to be saved by Jesus Christ. Therefore, as you move forward in your ministry as a catechetical leader, it can be very helpful to get in touch with your own story of Jesus' saving presence in your life.

## Tell Your Story

Before you go any further in exploring your role as a catechetical leader, take some time to pause and reflect on your relationship with Jesus as it has developed through your faith journey. A good way to do this is to focus on how the Lord has revealed his presence to you in certain key areas. Jot down a few thoughts in response to each question below.

| **Significant People** | **Moments of Joy** |
|---|---|
| Just as God spoke to his people through Moses and the prophets, God often speaks to us through other people. Who are the people in your life through whom the Lord has spoken? | By reflecting on moments of joy in our lives, we can recognize God's saving presence. What moments of joy come to mind now? How do they reveal God's saving presence in your life? |

| **Peak Moments of Grace** | **Milestones in Life** |
|---|---|
| Think of extraordinary moments when you felt you came face-to-face with the infinite—moments when God's presence was almost palpable. What do these moments tell you about God's saving power? | Think of major milestones in your life—a graduation, a new job, a promotion, a birthday or anniversary, or a wedding day—for which you are deeply grateful. What milestones in your life make you grateful to the Giver of all good gifts? |

## What It Means to Be a Disciple of Jesus

Baptism is much more than a call to live as a member of a community. It is a call to discipleship—to a life of actively following Jesus. Perhaps you've not thought of yourself as a disciple of Christ but only as a member of his church. One can be a member of the Church without living a life of discipleship. To be a disciple of Jesus is to choose an alternate way of living—one in which God reigns. It is a life marked by selfless love. It is a life marked by joy and hope—a confidence that, in God, all shall be well.

For many Catholics, discipleship is a relatively new concept, something more commonly spoken about in Protestant circles. In her book *Forming Intentional Disciples*, however, Sherry Weddell invites Catholics to change our thinking about discipleship. She invites us to realize that each of us—by virtue of our baptism—is called to enter intentionally into discipleship with Jesus Christ.

According to Weddell, "normative Catholicism" begins with having a conscious (intentional) and "explicit, personal attachment to Jesus Christ," or what she refers to as "personal discipleship." It is this living relationship—not just a religious identity—that we are called to communicate to others. Weddell explains that intentional discipleship begins with a decision to follow Jesus, just as Simon Peter decided to drop his nets and follow the Lord, not knowing what the future held. The U.S. Bishops agree: "Mature disciples make a conscious, firm decision," they write, "carried out in action, to be followers of Jesus Christ no matter the cost to themselves" (*Stewardship: A Disciple's Response*, USCCB). This "conscious, firm decision" to follow Jesus Christ springs from a belief that the Son of God who became human made it possible, through his own selfless suffering, Death, and Resurrection, for us to die to our own selfishness and to find new life in an alternate reality known as the Kingdom of God—a state of being in which God's will, manifested to us in Jesus Christ, reigns supreme.

As a catechetical leader and disciple of Jesus Christ, your primary role is to transmit a relationship that you yourself are actively participating in. According to St. John Paul II, the Good News that you are called to transmit "is directed to stirring a person to a conversion of heart and life and a clinging to Jesus Christ as Lord and Savior; to disposing a person to receive baptism and the Eucharist and to strengthen a person in the prospect and realization of new life according to the Spirit" (*Christifideles Laici*, 33).

## Living under the Influence of Jesus

To be a disciple of Jesus is to live under his influence. In other words, discipleship influences how we see ourselves, others, and God. As a catechetical leader—as someone who lives under the influence of Jesus—you are now living as someone who

- is in touch with your deepest desires
- has an awareness of and gratitude for God's unconditional love
- experiences God's nearness
- longs to be actively involved in God's work
- experiences intimacy with God
- no longer tries to save yourself
- seeks out others with whom to share the journey
- finds God in all things

- profoundly reveres each person as he or she is
- has a deep sense of gratitude
- lives as a person for others
- relies on Jesus to help you navigate the gray areas of life.

Suffice it to say, if you are a disciple of Jesus, you are a changed person. In my book *Under the Influence of Jesus: The Transforming Experience of Encountering Christ*, I put it this way:

> To admire Jesus from a distance is to misunderstand what he desires of us. Ultimately, Jesus is not to be admired from a distance: he is to be known on an intimate basis. Jesus does not ask Peter, "Do you have sufficient knowledge of all that I have said and done?" but rather, "Do you love me?"—a question that probes the deepest connection between human beings. Jesus does not desire *fans* who cheer from the sidelines but rather *friends* who will roll up their sleeves and work shoulder to shoulder with him to build the kingdom of God. (86)

Ultimately, this summarizes your response to Jesus' invitation to serve as a catechetical leader: you are not admiring Jesus from a distance but are delving deeper and deeper into an intimate relationship with him, one that is calling you to roll up your sleeves and work shoulder to shoulder with him to build his kingdom. "Being sent on a mission is a consequence of being a disciple" (*Stewardship: A Disciple's Response*, USCCB).

## Summary: They Left Their Nets

*At once they left their nets and followed him.* (Matt. 4:20, NIV)

Throughout Scripture, God calls and people respond. In baptism, God called you to a life of discipleship. Now, God has called you to deepen your discipleship through the service of catechetical ministry. This means that you have a vocation—and a vocation is something that needs to be nurtured and cared for. Your calling is unique, yet whenever God calls people, it is for the purpose of furthering the kingdom. As a disciple of Jesus, you are called to live under the influence of the Lord. As a catechetical leader, you are sent forth to call others to do the same as you create a culture of formation in your faith community.

## For Reflection and Discussion

- How does the term *vocation* change or deepen your understanding of your role as a catechetical leader?
- Recall the Scripture stories of people being called by God. Which one can you best relate to? Why?
- How would you tell your own story to encourage another person into the catechetical ministry?

## Growing as a Catechetical Leader

Living under the influence of Jesus is supposed to make a difference in our lives. Because you're a catechetical leader, people look to you to see how following Jesus has made a difference in your life so they can know what to expect in their own life. In what ways are you living under the influence of Jesus? What difference does it make in your life to be a disciple of Jesus? Can people see the difference?

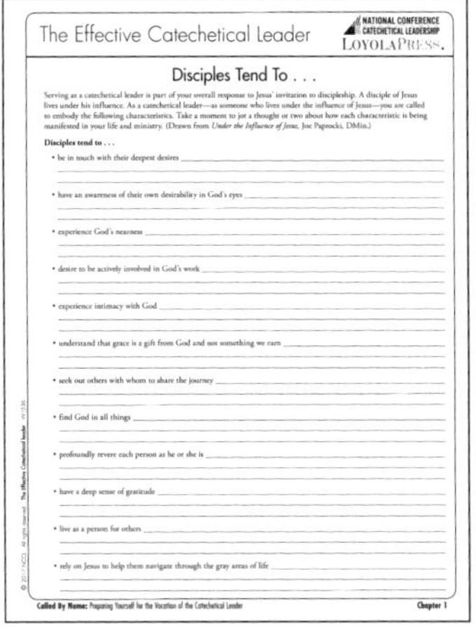

The Effective Catechetical Leader

NATIONAL CONFERENCE CATECHETICAL LEADERSHIP

LOYOLAPRESS.

**Disciples Tend To . . .**

Serving as a catechetical leader is part of your overall response to Jesus' invitation to discipleship. A disciple of Jesus lives under his influence. As a catechetical leader—as someone who lives under the influence of Jesus—you are called to embody the following characteristics. Take a moment to jot a thought or two about how each characteristic is being manifested in your life and ministry. (Drawn from *Under the Influence of Jesus*, Joe Paprocki, DMin.)

**Disciples tend to . . .**

- be in touch with their deepest desires
- have an awareness of their own desirability in God's eyes
- experience God's nearness
- desire to be actively involved in God's work
- experience intimacy with God
- understand that grace is a gift from God and not something we earn
- seek out others with whom to share the journey
- find God in all things
- profoundly revere each person as he or she is
- have a deep sense of gratitude
- live as a person for others
- rely on Jesus to help them navigate through the gray areas of life



**Called By Name:** Preparing Yourself for the Vocation of the Catechetical Leader — **Chapter 1**

Go to www.loyolapress.com/ECL to access the worksheet.

## Suggested Action

We said that creating a culture of faith formation is like setting up a controlled climate in a greenhouse to ensure that things grow properly. Every Sunday, after hearing the Gospel at Mass, decide on one or two actions you can take in the following week that will positively affect the "climate" of faith formation in your parish.

## For Further Consideration

To further explore the topic of this chapter, consider the following resources:

*Forming Intentional Disciples.* Sherry Weddell (Huntington, IN: Our Sunday Visitor, 2012).

*Under the Influence of Jesus: The Transforming Experience of Encountering Christ.* Joe Paprocki (Chicago: Loyola Press, 2014).

*Stewardship: A Disciple's Response.* The United States Conference of Catholic Bishops.

National Certification Standards for Lay Ecclesial Ministers by The Alliance for the Certification of Ecclesial Ministry, 2011.

# 2

# Disciples in Action: God's Mission, the Church, and the Ministry of Catechesis

Some years ago, a movie titled *That Thing You Do!* produced a hit song of the same name. In the song, the singer laments his lost love. "I try and try to forget you, girl," he croons. "But it's just so hard to do. / Every time you do that thing you do." The phrase *do that thing you do* came to mind recently as I listened to a webinar on the New Evangelization by my good friend Jonathan Sullivan. In the webinar, Jonathan described local parishes as "places where people gather to do what disciples do." As a catechetical leader, you've been called to train people to do what disciples do. But just what *is* that thing?

## That Thing You Do

In *The 7 Habits of Highly Effective People*, Stephen Covey claims that one thing highly effective people do is "begin with the end in mind." Doing this, he writes, "means to start with a clear understanding of your destination. It means to know where you're going so that you better understand where you are now and so that the steps you take are always in the right direction." Beginning with the end in mind is one of the things highly effective disciples do, too. But this raises yet another question: Where are we going?

The end of the Mass—when we are told to "Go in peace, glorifying the Lord by your life"—gives us a clue. It's no coincidence that the word *Mass* comes from the Concluding Rites of the liturgy. In Latin, the words of the dismissal are *Ite! Missa est!* meaning, "Go! You are dismissed!" It is from this word *missa* that we have the word *Mass*. We indeed begin with the end in mind. We are sent forth at the end of the Mass to leave the safety and security of the sanctuary and to partake in a mission. "Go" means internalizing the word of God and going forth to proclaim it, in both word and deed, to others who may not be completely receptive to hearing or experiencing it. "Go," we are urged. It is the only way that Jesus Christ will reach those who have not joined us in worship and in prayer. Too many choose not to worship with us, so we must go to them instead of waiting for them to come to us.

So, the primary venue for the "thing we do" as disciples is not the parish but the world. We gather at the parish to be equipped to go forth and carry out the mission of Christ, which is to bring all people to the Father. It is important for us to remember that the church, per se, does not have a mission. God has a mission and that mission has a church. Simply put, a mission is a task or an assignment, usually of significance. A mission statement is a concise articulation of purpose—a reason for doing that thing we do. God's mission is to gather all people to himself through his Son, Jesus Christ, in the Holy Spirit. Knowing this mission, your role as a catechetical leader is to help people remain focused on the tasks of discipleship and to encourage them to be creative and innovative in carrying out this mission.

Sent by Jesus Christ and guided by his Spirit, we are entrusted with this mission of inviting people to a friendship with God—a relationship that brings God close to each of us. As a catechetical leader, your role is to coordinate the efforts of the parish community to introduce people to Jesus and to assist them in deepening their relationship with him through discipleship. Your task is not primarily to transmit ideas but rather to foster encounters with a Person—Jesus Christ.

## Relationships Change Us

Throughout your life, you have no doubt made many friends and entered more than a few serious relationships. Thus, you know that relationships change us. In fact, to enter a relationship with the notion that we will not change is to doom the relationship to failure. When we invite others into our lives, we need to make room for them. For starters, we change by making time for them—time that was once for ourselves. We make room for their ideas, desires, and dreams and expect that they will do the same. We find ourselves developing new interests and participating in new activities. We begin to integrate some of our friends' values, behaviors, and attitudes while also remaining true to ourselves. We may find ourselves eliminating bad habits that might repel our friends and developing new habits that might draw them closer.

In the movie *As Good as It Gets*, Melvin, a cranky, obsessive-compulsive author (played by Jack Nicholson) seems to be totally incapable of expressing a kind thought to anyone. This becomes problematic, however, when he finds himself attracted to a waitress named Carol (played by Helen Hunt) but is unable to say anything kind in her presence. Finally, he works up the courage to take her out to dinner and announces that he has a great compliment to give her. He explains that, although his "shrink" told him he needed to take medication, he really, really hates pills. However, he admits that after meeting Carol, he did start taking the pills. Baffled, Carol says, "I don't quite get how that's a compliment for me." After a brief pause, Melvin explains, "You make me want to be a better man." Often, when we encounter someone with qualities we admire, we become more aware of our own shortcomings, which sparks a new desire for improvement.

Becoming a disciple of Jesus works the same way. When we accept Jesus' invitation to discipleship, we encounter his great mercy, which in turn makes us more aware of our own shortcomings and our desire to be better people. We cannot help but ask for forgiveness and for the grace we need to move forward. Walking with Jesus makes us want to be better people. "Sucking in" our flabby spiritual gut, however, is not the solution: at some point, we have to breathe freely. The only authentic response to encountering Jesus, therefore, is true and lasting conversion, or transformation.

This is where you come in as the catechetical leader. You are a facilitator of encounters and conversions. In his apostolic exhortation *Evangelii Gaudium*, Pope Francis explains how this conversion is at the heart of our evangelization efforts: "It is impossible to persevere in a fervent evangelization," he writes, "unless we are convinced from personal experience that it is not the same thing to have known Jesus as not to have known him, not the same thing to walk with him as to walk blindly, not the same thing to hear his word as not to know it, and not the same thing to contemplate him, to worship him, to find our peace in him, as not to."

## Six Transformative Aspects of the Good News of Jesus

The mission of the Church, and therefore the task of catechetical leadership, can be compared to the task of a campaign worker who has met the candidate, feels changed by his or her message, and wants to introduce others to this candidate in the hope of creating a movement. We don't accomplish the mission of the Church by indoctrinating others with concepts but by introducing them to a Person. We do this by describing our own encounters with this Person—Jesus Christ—and explaining how he has changed us. In other words, we tell a story that holds out the promise of something better.

In an article in *Catechetical Leader* magazine, Nick Wagner of Team RCIA identifies "Six Amazing Things Every RCIA Inquirer Has to Learn." I would argue that these are six amazing things every Catholic needs to know. We tend to assume that people know what the Good News of Jesus is all about when in fact many are unable to articulate it. Nick synthesizes the essence of the Good News as follows:

1. God is not an absent Father. (God is here, now, loving you unconditionally.)
2. There's nothing to be afraid of. (God saves us from darkness and fear.)
3. God brings justice and righteousness. (God is always just, fair, and righteous.)
4. Jesus is a big deal. (Jesus completely reveals God to us.)
5. We are a big deal too. (Disciples reveal Jesus to the world.)
6. It only gets better from here. (We're on a path to perfect joy.)

The role of the catechetical leader is to emphasize these core principles, which are at the heart of everything we teach.

## Every Leader Needs a Vision

Dr. Martin Luther King Jr. famously proclaimed, "I have a dream!" Inspired by Scripture, Dr. King shared a vision of a world in which people would "not be judged by the color of their skin, but by the content of their character." His vision has inspired generations of people to work for the transformation of society. Every leader—including a catechetical leader—needs a vision. Without one, a leader is like a travel agent: he or she can provide you with information about a place without ever having visited it. Leaders *with* a vision, however, are much more like tour guides. They have already been on the journey, recognize what is required to make it, know the attractions that mustn't be missed, can point out dangers and obstacles, and can articulate what the journey means to them personally. In your role as a catechetical leader, you are called to be a tour guide, not a travel agent. This means that you must have a vision of the journey to the kingdom based on experience so that you can guide others to embark on a journey of their own.

The vision that is placed before us comes from our Lord Jesus Christ and is articulated most profoundly in the Sermon on the Mount (Matthew 5—7): Jesus' very own "keynote address." In this discourse, Jesus describes a realm in which

- it is blessed to be poor, meek, and merciful;
- it is blessed to mourn, to hunger and thirst for justice, to work for peace, and to be persecuted for God's sake;
- anger is not an acceptable motivator;
- the other cheek is turned;
- all people, including enemies, are loved;
- good deeds are done in private;
- God is spoken to as a Father who is near and not distant; and
- worry and judgment have no place.

This is Jesus' vision—and it comes from his great and even wild imagination. Unfortunately, imagination often gets a bad rap as being out of touch with reality. In fact, imagination is the prerequisite of hope. It is the capacity to see *through* reality to an alternate and even greater reality. Imagination helps us navigate, decipher, and transcend the reality that meets the eye so that we can recognize unseen reality. Imagination is not foolishness. As a catechetical leader, you are called to be a person of vision—someone with a great and even wild imagination who can "see" the Kingdom of God.

Ultimately, Jesus' wildly imaginative proclamation of the kingdom of God is much more than the proposal of a *preferred* way of seeing reality. Rather, Jesus' proclamation is an *indispensable* way of seeing reality. Catechesis helps people see beyond the present reality of dashed hopes to an alternate reality that holds the promise of possibilities.

## The Good Kind of Heartburn

The promise of possibilities is precisely what the risen Christ helped the two disciples on the road to Emmaus see. The disciples' despair over Jesus' crucifixion had impaired their vision and rendered them incapable of recognizing the man walking with them. Jesus listened to their story and then challenged them to see things differently as he guided them through Scripture. "Did not the Messiah have to suffer these things and then enter his glory?" he reminded them. Finally, when he sat down at the table with them and broke bread, their eyes were opened and they recognized the risen Lord in their midst, exclaiming, "Were not our hearts burning within us while he was talking to us on the road?" (Luke 24:32). Jesus gave them heartburn—the kind of heartburn you want to keep.

Throughout the church's history, the Holy Spirit has enkindled in the hearts of numerous people a passionate desire to share the Good News of Jesus with others. Your role as a catechetical leader is to join their ranks and to give people heartburn—to foster in them a vision of a future filled not with despair and endings but with hope and new beginnings. In Ignatian spirituality, this sense of holy hope is referred to as "something more" (in Latin, *magis*): the abiding desire for a greater good that can be found only in God.

Nurturing a desire for "something more" is not easy in a world filled with indifference, distraction, cynicism, and relativism—all of which diminish the human spirit rather than enlarge it. For you to tackle this challenge as a catechetical leader, you must do everything in your power to become and remain a person of vision—of a great and wild imagination. "But where should I begin?" you might be wondering. Here are a few concrete suggestions for right-brain activities that will stimulate your imagination. (You can read more about these in my book *7 Keys to Spiritual Wellness*.)

- Turn off the TV.
- Read, especially fiction and biographies.
- Focus on humor.
- Draw or paint a picture.
- Peruse works of art.
- Work with your hands.
- Listen to music and sing.
- Engage in a hobby.
- Exercise regularly, eat well, and get enough sleep.
- Break your patterns and be illogical on occasion.
- Keep an idea notebook, or write in a journal.
- Attend the theater.
- Rearrange your work space or living space.
- Meditate.
- Practice deep breathing.
- Learn a new language.
- Associate with creative people.
- Cook or bake something.
- Do some decorating or remodeling.
- Travel or do armchair traveling.
- Interact with children.
- Play board games that require strategy.

All these activities can awaken our imagination, which in turn sparks the fire that fuels a healthy spirituality. Through his great imagination, Jesus envisions a world in which the hungry are fed, the thirsty are given drink, the sick are tended to, the homeless are sheltered, the imprisoned are visited, the naked are clothed, and the estranged are welcomed. The God you proclaim as a catechetical leader is on fire, has a vision and a mission, and has called you to invite others to help set the whole world on fire.

## Summary: Go and Make Disciples

*[Jesus said,] "Go therefore and make disciples of all nations, baptizing them in the name of the Father and of the Son and of the Holy Spirit, and teaching them to obey everything that I have commanded you."*
(Matt. 28:19–20)

You are being sent. To borrow a phrase from the movie *The Blues Brothers*, you're "on a mission from God." This is what disciples of Jesus do: they go forth to carry out God's mission of drawing all people to himself. As a catechetical leader, you are now participating in a formal way in this mission, inviting people to encounter Jesus Christ and helping them to recognize that this encounter is transformative. The reality that Jesus envisioned and described in his Sermon on the Mount—the reality that is the kingdom of God—is not how today's world looks, and many are unable to imagine or envision that reality taking shape. It is your responsibility to be a person of great imagination—someone capable of seeing God's reality and helping others to see it as well. In the words of the U.S. bishops, "Jesus came to set this fire upon the earth, until all is ablaze in the love of God. We pray this fire will come upon us as disciples as we, led by the Spirit, carry out Christ's great commission to go and make disciples of all the nations" (*Go and Make Disciples*, USCCB).

## For Reflection and Discussion

- What does it mean to you to say, "God has a mission and that mission has a church"? How would you describe this mission to someone?
- The essence of the Good News is that God's unconditional love is ours for the taking (and sharing). As a catechetical leader, how can you effectively and practically proclaim this Good News to others?

## Growing as a Catechetical Leader

We said earlier that in your role as a catechetical leader, you are called to be a tour guide, not just a travel agent. This implies that you have some familiarity with the kingdom to which we are called. Jesus described this reality—the kingdom of God—in his Sermon on the Mount (Matt. 5—7). What aspects of life in the kingdom are you most eager to share with others? What aspects do you find most difficult to explain?

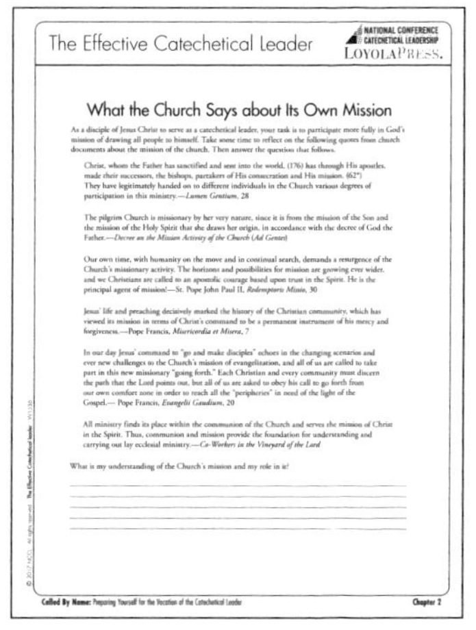

The Effective Catechetical Leader

NATIONAL CONFERENCE CATECHETICAL LEADERSHIP

LOYOLAPRESS.

What the Church Says about Its Own Mission

As a disciple of Jesus Christ to serve as a catechetical leader, your task is to participate more fully in God's mission of drawing all people to himself. Take some time to reflect on the following quotes from church documents about the mission of the church. Then answer the question that follows.

> Christ, whom the Father has sanctified and sent into the world, (176) has through His apostles, made their successors, the bishops, partakers of His consecration and His mission. (62*) They have legitimately handed on to different individuals in the Church various degrees of participation in this ministry.—*Lumen Gentium*, 28

> The pilgrim Church is missionary by her very nature, since it is from the mission of the Son and the mission of the Holy Spirit that she draws her origin, in accordance with the decree of God the Father.—*Decree on the Mission Activity of the Church (Ad Gentes)*

> Our own time, with humanity on the move and in continual search, demands a resurgence of the Church's missionary activity. The horizons and possibilities for mission are growing ever wider, and we Christians are called to an apostolic courage based upon trust in the Spirit. He is the principal agent of mission!—St. Pope John Paul II, *Redemptoris Missio*, 30

> Jesus' life and preaching decisively marked the history of the Christian community, which has viewed its mission in terms of Christ's command to be a permanent instrument of his mercy and forgiveness.—Pope Francis, *Misericordia et Misera*, 7

> In our day Jesus' command to "go and make disciples" echoes in the changing scenarios and ever new challenges to the Church's mission of evangelization, and all of us are called to take part in this new missionary "going forth." Each Christian and every community must discern the path that the Lord points out, but all of us are asked to obey his call to go forth from our own comfort zone in order to reach all the "peripheries" in need of the light of the Gospel.— Pope Francis, *Evangelii Gaudium*, 20

> All ministry finds its place within the communion of the Church and serves the mission of Christ in the Spirit. Thus, communion and mission provide the foundation for understanding and carrying out lay ecclesial ministry.—*Co-Workers in the Vineyard of the Lord*

What is my understanding of the Church's mission and my role in it?



**Called By Name:** Preparing Yourself for the Vocation of the Catechetical Leader — **Chapter 2**

Go to www.loyolapress.com/ECL to access the worksheet.

## Suggested Action

To envision the kingdom of God to which you are calling people, you must be a person of great imagination. Commit to practicing some of the suggestions for stimulating your imagination given in the section "The Good Kind of Heartburn."

## For Further Consideration

To further explore the topic of this chapter, consider the following resources:

*Evangelii Nuntiandi: Apostolic Exhortation.* Pope Paul VI (1975) and *Evangelii Gaudium: Apostolic Exhortation on the Proclamation of the Gospel in Today's World.* Pope Francis (2013).

*Forming Intentional Disciples in the Parish: A Webinar.* Jonathan F. Sullivan (Leadership Institute/USCCB—www.usccb.org)

*Go and Make Disciples: A National Plan and Strategy for Catholic Evangelization in the United States.* The USCCB (Washington, D.C., 1992).

# 3

# You Are Called by Name: The Vocation of the Parish Catechetical Leader

Most likely, you fall into one of the following four categories:

- You are discerning the call to catechetical leadership;
- You have recently become a catechetical leader and are discerning whether you've made the right decision;
- You have been a catechetical leader for some time but are discerning whether to continue in this ministry;
- You have been a catechetical leader for some time and are discerning ways to grow in your ministry.

Wherever you fall, you are a discerning individual! Serving as a catechetical leader is no ordinary job; it is a vocation to which you have been called, and vocations involve discernment.

## Here I Am; Send Me!

In the past, many Catholics believed that vocations were only for priests and religious. Since the Second Vatican Council, however, the church has emphasized that every human being has a vocation—a calling from God to more closely reflect the divine image. In a document called *Guide for Catechists*, the Catholic Church says the following:

> Every baptized Catholic is personally called by the Holy Spirit to make his or her contribution to the coming of God's kingdom. Within the lay state there are various *vocations*, or different spiritual and apostolic roads to be followed by both individuals and groups. Within the general vocation of the laity there are particular ones. At the origin of the catechist's vocation, therefore, apart from the sacraments of Baptism and Confirmation, there is a specific call from the Holy Spirit, a "*special charism recognized by the Church*" and made explicit by the Bishop's mandate. It is important for the catechist candidate to recognize the supernatural and ecclesial significance of this call, so as to be able to respond, like the Son of God, "*Here I come*" (*Heb* 10:7), or, like the prophet, "*Here I am; send me*" (*Is* 6:8).

This passage includes some mighty powerful thoughts for you to dwell on. First, while all of God's people have a vocation, you have chosen a "particular" path in response to a specific call from the Holy Spirit. Second, you have a "special charism recognized by the Church"—a gift for leadership in the Church's catechetical mission. Third, your call has "supernatural and ecclesial significance," which means that you have been called to enter more deeply into the mystery of God and the Body of Christ. And you thought this was just a job!

## It Starts with a Call to Holiness

The people of Israel recognized that they had been called by God. In the Old Testament, we read:

- "I am the LORD, I have called you in righteousness" (Isa. 42:6).
- "I have called you by name, you are mine" (Isa. 43:1).
- "When Israel was a child, I loved him, and out of Egypt I called my son" (Hosea 11:1).

Jesus, in turn, called disciples (and the apostles) to follow him, echoing the Father's call to his chosen people. Later, St. Paul reminded early Christians in Rome that we are "called to belong to Jesus Christ" (Rom. 1:6).

Today the Church continues the tradition: we view ourselves as called by God in baptism to be his people, to live holy lives and to spread the light of the gospel throughout the world. While there are particular vocations in the Church—such as priesthood, religious life, married life, and single life—our initial call comes to us through baptism, and this initial call to holiness is the most important vocation of all. The bishops of the Second Vatican Council emphasized this. "All in the Church," they wrote, "whether they belong to the hierarchy or are cared for by it, are called to holiness" (*Constitution of the Church*, ch. 5).

The message is clear: we are called to be a holy people and to live out that holiness in whatever circumstances occur. You are being called to live out this holiness as a catechetical leader.

## What Does Holiness "Look Like"?

We all hope and pray that we will find friends (and especially spouses) who are the "real thing." We sometimes say people who are the "real thing" are *authentic*. Ultimately, that's what holiness is all about—being authentic. For over two thousand years, countless Christians have sought to live holy lives by entering relationship with the most authentic person in history: Jesus Christ. In the Creed, we say that Jesus is "God from God, light from light, true God from true God." We also say that he was "incarnate of the Virgin Mary and became man" and that he "suffered death"—"was crucified, died, and was buried." He is the real thing. He is authentically human and authentically divine.

Jesus' love is authentic, too. How do we know? Because he gave his life for us. Real love is unselfish and wants nothing in return. That's the kind of love that God offers to us. God's love is selfless and unconditional. It is sheer, authentic gift.

That's what it means to be holy: to give authentic, unconditional love to others, just as God does to us. Sometimes when we hear the word *holy*, we imagine a state of perfection. But that's not what holiness is. God isn't calling us to be perfect but to be authentic—to live as an authentic follower of Jesus.

This is a tall order today because so much of our world is *not* authentic. It's much easier to be phony or fake. But in the Christian tradition, holiness begins and ends with saying that you believe Jesus is the real thing and that you want to live as his authentic follower. It means saying no to all the selfish, deceptive, and phony stuff Satan has to offer—stuff that looks good on the surface and feels good as well but ultimately causes us to "miss the mark" (which is the literal meaning of the word *sin*).

It's no coincidence that at baptism—the ritual that enables us to set sail on a journey toward holiness—the first question the priest asks is, "Do you reject Satan, and all his works, and all his empty promises?" The journey to holiness begins with the sobering reminder that without intervention, we will continue hopelessly to miss the mark. Baptism is that intervention. But like any intervention in life, it isn't a quick fix. There isn't any magic involved. It is simply the watershed moment: a first step to admitting that we need help and opening ourselves up to the grace that heals. That's why we Catholics so often renew our baptismal promises at Mass: we need to remain vigilant, listen for God's voice, and frequently reject Satan, because he doesn't go away.

## How Do I Listen for "God's Voice"?

While it would be nice to hear a powerful, heavenly voice call you by name and say, "I want you to be a catechetical leader!" it tends not to work that way. In fact, we are usually skeptical of anyone who claims they literally hear God's voice. For most of us, that's just not how it happens. God is much subtler than that—which is exactly the point of the story of Elijah, who encounters God not in an earthquake and not in a fire but in a gentle whisper (1 Kings 19).

Here are just a few of the channels through which God subtly speaks to us. As you continue to reflect on, discern, and nurture your vocation to serve as a catechetical leader, try to pay closer attention to them.

- **Thoughts.** In response to our prayer for guidance, God may plant a recurring thought in our mind. It might continue to rattle around until we pay attention to it.
- **Memories.** God might stir up memories from our past to speak to us about something happening in the present.
- **Feelings.** It is important to pay attention to any feelings that arise during prayer. God may give you a feeling of peace and contentment to remind you of his presence, or he may give you a feeling of restlessness to move you to action.
- **Hopes and desires.** At times, God speaks to us by awakening hopes and desires within us. We may find ourselves growing more aware of a yearning that has long been dim or dormant, or we might experience a yearning we've never had before. When people say that they are "going with their gut feeling," they often mean they are following an inner hope or desire.
- **Dreams.** God has always spoken to people in dreams. In *Dreams: God's Forgotten Language*, John Sanford encourages us to pay attention to images that come from our unconscious self as clues to important insights. Dreams should not be taken as literal

messages from God, but they can reveal God's movement deep within us through symbols, concepts, or emotions.

- **Nature.** At times Catholics are suspicious of the notion that God speaks to us through nature, because it smacks of New Age spirituality or the ancient yet persistent heresy of pantheism. Catholics do not equate nature with God, but we do believe that nature carries God's fingerprints and reflects his presence, goodness, strength, power, and beauty. In the encyclical *Laudato Si'*, Pope Francis reminds us that "the entire material universe speaks of God's love, his boundless affection for us. Soil, water, mountains: everything is, as it were, a caress of God" (84).
- **Experiences.** God's message for us may be wrapped in an everyday experience or, less often, in an extraordinary one. Reflecting on our experiences is an important way of recognizing what God may be saying to us or asking of us.
- **Encounters with others.** Throughout Scripture, God uses people as his mouthpieces, and he continues to do so today. God constantly speaks to us through other people's words and actions. By paying closer attention to the people with whom we live, work, serve, and play, we may discover God speaking to us.
- **Encounters with beauty.** God speaks to us every time we experience beauty. Beauty may come to us in the form of music, drama, literature, athletics, art, culture, and even the face of a loved one. Beauty provokes feelings within us, and very often those feelings are part of a wordless conversation with God.

Our communication with God often occurs through channels beyond words. Therefore, we need a kind of antenna to receive these subtle messages. We need to practice discernment—involving God in our decision-making—so that we can tell whether a message is coming from God, from our self, or from a voice we shouldn't be listening to.

## But How Do I Know It's God's Voice?

As we have noted, to be a catechetical leader is to have a vocation—a call from God. The church reminds us,

> The vocation of the laity to catechesis springs from the sacrament of Baptism. It is strengthened by the Sacrament of Confirmation. Through the Sacraments of Baptism and Confirmation, they participate in the priestly, prophetic and kingly ministry of Christ. In addition to the common vocation of the apostolate, some people feel called interiorly by God to assume the service of catechist. The Church awakens and discerns this divine vocation and confers the mission to catechize. (*General Directory for Catechesis*, 231)

To have a vocation to catechetical leadership means that at every step of the way, you need to involve God in your decision making. We call this *discernment*. It's important to know that your vocation and the discernment involved in it are not "once and done" experiences. God didn't call you once. God calls you each and every day. Your vocation to live a life of holiness is something that you continue to nurture and discern every day of your life. It is an ongoing response to God's invitation to serve.

Many choices we face in life are very complex. How do we know what God wants us to do? What is God's will for us? This is where discernment comes into play. Discernment refers to the process of aligning ourselves with God's will to learn what God is calling us to. Discernment is needed not only in immediate decisions (*Should I say something to my best friend about his drinking?*) but also in decisions about the overall direction of our lives (*Should I accept this promotion even though it means relocating?*). Both kinds of decisions have everything to do with God and the kind of person God is calling us to be. Every choice we make, no matter how small, is an opportunity to align ourselves with God's will.

Here are some tried-and-true strategies for discerning how God may be calling you.

- **Talk to someone you respect.** God often speaks to us through the wisdom of others. Seek out at least one person you feel has the gift of wisdom and ask for his or her advice.
- **Find some solitude.** It's good to talk to others when making an important decision, but at some point, it is crucial to make time to be alone with your thoughts and with God. Consciously invite God into your decision-making process.
- **Start with what you know.** Lay out all the facts in front of you so that you can deal with the known before you delve into the unknown!
- **Consult the community.** Ministry is rooted in the community of the baptized. Invite others in the church to discern with you how your gifts might be of best service to others.
- **Tell God what you desire and what you fear.** Be honest. Tell God your deepest desires and fears related to this situation. Before you can say the words *thy will be done,* it's important to understand what your own will is.
- **Let God speak to you.** As we have observed, most of us don't hear an audible voice when God speaks to us. But God does speak in other ways. What kinds of thoughts, feelings (especially love, joy, peace, or a lack thereof), and memories might God be stirring within you to guide your decision? What Scripture story or saint's life comes to mind that might enlighten you? Find the passage or story and read it prayerfully.
- **Know that God has a plan for you.** Remind yourself that you are not on your own and that you don't have to yell and scream to get God's attention in this matter. On the contrary, God has a plan for you, and his plan is driven purely by love.

- **Pray to do God's will.** As difficult as it may be, pray the words *thy will be done.* Ask God to give you the strength you need to continue to discern his will and to follow it.
- **Wait.** If circumstances allow, wait before making your decision. Continue to pay attention to your feelings to see which direction you are drawn to.
- **Prayerfully commit.** At some point, you need to act. Knowing that you have sought God's will, set out to do the loving thing.
- **Check out the fruits.** Discernment is ongoing. After you make a decision and act on it, prayerfully evaluate what has happened. If the fruits or outcomes of your decision are good, the decision you made is probably good. If the fruits are "rotten," you may need to alter your course. True discernment results in good fruit—even if it takes the shape of something we normally wouldn't consider.

Discernment can help you when you face decisions and as you continue to ponder the call to serve as a catechetical leader. Even though making good decisions can be difficult, trust that the Holy Spirit is with you to guide you and help you choose what is good and true. By tuning in to God's voice and adjusting the frequency to make a connection to a language beyond words, you can nurture your vocation as a catechetical leader.

## But Why Me, and Why Catechetical Leadership?

Throughout Scripture, people who encounter God's call tend to react with surprise, confusion, fear, and even reluctance. A good example of such a reaction is found in Luke's Gospel, when Elizabeth responds to a visit from her pregnant cousin Mary by asking, "Why has this happened to me, that the mother of my Lord comes to me?" (Luke 1:43). Perhaps you had a similar reaction when the idea of catechetical leadership first visited you. "Who am I that God would call me to serve in this ministry?" you might have asked.

The truth is this: God does not call the qualified but qualifies the called. This means that God—and the church—recognizes within you the capacity to carry out certain responsibilities. Fortunately, these responsibilities, or competencies, have been spelled out for us in the *National Certification Standards for Lay Ecclesial Ministers*. These competencies include

- directing the parish catechetical program through design, implementation, and evaluation of parish catechetical processes.
- implementing the catechumenate model as inspiration for catechesis in age-appropriate ways.
- developing a comprehensive lifelong vision and plan for parish catechesis based on ecclesial catechetical documents.
- ensuring the centrality of catechesis in the development of the parish as an evangelizing and catechizing community.
- developing and implementing parish catechetical policies in accord with (arch)diocesan policies and guidelines.
- providing orientation and in-servicing of catechetical committee members and formation teams in their areas of responsibility.
- exercising effective supervision of catechetical employees and volunteers while fostering leadership abilities.

The role to which you have been called is both ancient and new. Since the beginning of the church, members of the faith community have stepped forward to facilitate the faithful transmission of the gospel to each generation. For many centuries, however, this task was understood as the purview of clergy and religious. Since the Second Vatican Council, the Church has been engaged in the task of calling the laity to assume co-responsibility with the clergy and religious in ministerial tasks. Over time, the role of catechetical leader has developed a greater professionalism and legitimacy while also cultivating a deeper ministerial identity. Today the church describes the presence of a professionally trained catechetical leader as "the single most critical factor in an effective parish catechetical program" (*National Directory for Catechesis*, 54 B–5). Your response to the call to serve in this capacity embodies the spirit of the words of St. Pope John Paul II:

> A new state of affairs today both in the Church and in social, economic, political and cultural life, calls with a particular urgency for the action of the lay faithful. If lack of commitment is always unacceptable, the present time renders it even more so. *It is not permissible for anyone to remain idle.* (*Christifideles Laici*, 3)

Remaining idle is one thing you will never have to worry about as a catechetical leader!

## Summary: I Call You by Name

> *But now thus says the LORD,*
> *he who created you, O Jacob,*
> *he who formed you, O Israel:*
> *"Do not fear, for I have redeemed you;*
> *I have called you by name, you are mine."* (Isa. 43:1)

Using the word *vocation* to describe your role as catechetical leader comes with implications. First and foremost, it implies that God is involved and that you are responding to God's initiative. It also implies that God is calling you to something specific, beginning with the call to holiness—the call to life as an authentic disciple of Jesus. In order to hear this calling, which is ongoing, you need to listen for God's "voice," which comes to us in ways beyond words—often in thoughts, feelings, memories, experiences, and so on. In order to pay closer attention to God's subtle voice, you need to practice discernment. Your vocation as a catechetical leader is a response to the ever-changing landscape of the church—a "new state of affairs"—and its desire to meet the needs of God's people. Your call is urgent. You are responding to needs that require immediate attention.

## For Reflection and Discussion

- What does it mean for you to be holy? To be authentic? Who are people you know whom you consider holy and authentic? What traits of theirs can be imitated?
- How do you "hear" God's voice? What are some ways beyond words that God has spoken and continues to speak to you?

## Growing as a Catechetical Leader

To help others discern their vocation, you must constantly reflect on your own vocation. Of all the channels through which God "speaks" to us—thoughts, feelings, memories, hopes and desires, dreams, nature, experiences, encounters with people, and encounters with beauty—which played the largest part in your vocational discernment as a catechetical leader? To which do you need to pay more attention as you move forward?

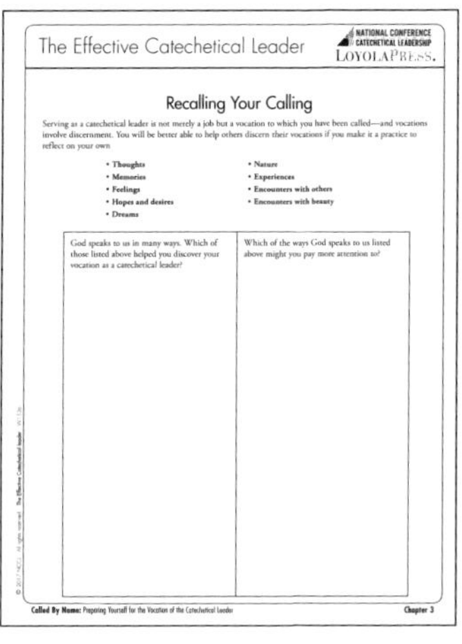

The Effective Catechetical Leader

NATIONAL CONFERENCE CATECHETICAL LEADERSHIP

LOYOLAPRESS.

Recalling Your Calling

Serving as a catechetical leader is not merely a job but a vocation to which you have been called—and vocations involve discernment. You will be better able to help others discern their vocations if you make it a practice to reflect on your own

- **Thoughts**
- **Memories**
- **Feelings**
- **Hopes and desires**
- **Dreams**
- **Nature**
- **Experiences**
- **Encounters with others**
- **Encounters with beauty**

| God speaks to us in many ways. Which of those listed above helped you discover your vocation as a catechetical leader? | Which of the ways God speaks to us listed above might you pay more attention to? |
| --- | --- |

**Called By Name:** Preparing Yourself for the Vocation of the Catechetical Leader — **Chapter 3**

Go to www.loyolapress.com/ECL to access the worksheet.

## Suggested Action

An important part of discernment is talking things over with a trusted friend or colleague. Make it a regular habit to spend time with such a person. Invite him or her to help you sort things out and keep your perspective. You might also consider the benefits of regular spiritual direction, something we'll talk more about in chapter 5.

## For Further Consideration

To further explore the topic of this chapter, consider the following resources:

*The Catechist's Backpack: Spiritual Essentials for the Journey.* Joe Paprocki and Julianne Stanz (Chicago: Loyola Press, 2015).

*Just Ministry: Professional Ethics for Pastoral Ministers.* Richard M. Gula (Mahwah, NJ: Paulist Press, 2010).

*Christifideles Laici: Apostolic Exhortation on the Vocation and the Mission of the Lay Faithful in the Church and in the World.* St. Pope John Paul II (1988).

*God's Voice Within: The Ignatian Way to Discover God's Will.* Mark Thibodeaux (Chicago: Loyola Press, 2010).

# 4

# The Three-Dimensional Parish Catechetical Leader: Being, Knowing, Doing

You may be familiar with a little guy known as Flat Stanley. Based on a series of children's books from the early 1960s and popularized by a schoolteacher in the mid-1990s, Flat Stanley is a paper doll that kids take with them on trips to various destinations and photograph in front of famous landmarks. The photos are then shared so that kids around the world can develop a greater global awareness and cultivate their storytelling skills. Flat Stanley is fun and engaging. There's only one problem with Flat Stanley.

He's flat.

## Don't Be Flat

While being flat has enabled Stanley to squeeze into small spaces and travel the world, flatness is not generally considered a desirable trait. No one likes food that tastes flat or a carbonated drink that has gone flat. No one likes singing or musical instruments that are flat. No one likes a character or a plot that is flat. In general, being thought of as flat is something to be avoided. The same holds true for catechetical ministers—especially parish catechetical leaders. You are called to be well rounded. Unlike Flat Stanley, who gets by just fine in a two-dimensional world, a parish catechetical leader is called to be formed in three dimensions.

According to the *General Directory for Catechesis*,

> The formation of catechists is made up of different dimensions. The deepest dimension refers to the very being of the catechist, to his human and Christian dimension. Formation, above all else, must help him to mature as a person, a believer and as an apostle. This is what the catechist must know to be able to fulfill his responsibilities well. This dimension is permeated by the double commitment he has to the message and to man. It requires the catechist to have a sufficient knowledge of the message that he transmits and of those to whom he transmits the message and of the social context in which they live. This then is the dimension of *savoir-faire*, of knowing how to transmit the message, so that it is an act of communication. (238)

In essence, the three dimensions of formation for catechetical leaders are *being*, *knowing*, and *doing*—being a disciple of Christ, knowing the gospel message, and doing the work of communicating it. Let's take a look at each of these dimensions in turn.

## Being, Knowing, and Doing

Let's work in reverse order so that we can devote most of our attention to the aspect of *being*.

Formation in the dimension of *doing* gives catechetical ministers the skills to proclaim the gospel effectively and to articulate a clear vision for the faith-formation program. To accomplish these main goals, a catechetical leader must *do* a wide variety of smaller tasks, including the following:

- Build relationships
- Collaborate with others
- Handle conflict
- Make decisions
- Build community
- Delegate responsibility

- Supervise others
- Design, implement, and evaluate curriculum
- Select textbooks
- Use social media
- Recruit, train, and form catechists
- Keep records
- Maintain a budget
- Communicate effectively
- Facilitate meetings
- Advocate for the catechetical ministry

Formation in the dimension of *knowing* helps catechetical leaders gain sufficient knowledge of the Catholic faith, of catechetical principles, and of organizational development and leadership theory. Among the many things that a parish catechetical leader needs to know are

- Catholic doctrine (as it relates to the Creeds, Christology, ecclesiology, Mary and the saints, the sacraments, liturgy, morality, social justice, Catholic social teaching, and prayer)
- Catechetical documents (*Catechism of the Catholic Church*, *General Directory for Catechesis*, *National Directory for Catechesis*, *Our Hearts Were Burning Within Us*, *Catechesi Tradendae*, *Renewing the Vision*, *Go and Make Disciples*)
- Papal encyclicals and apostolic exhortations such as *Redemptoris Missio*, *Deus Caritas Est*, and *Evangelii Gaudium*
- Catechetical models
- Catechetical resources (including textbooks, video, digital)
- Diocesan structures
- Local and national catechetical organizations such as the National Conference for Catechetical Leadership (NCCL), the National Association for Lay Ministry (NALM), the National Federation for Catholic Youth Ministry (NFCYM), the National Catholic Education Association (NCEA), and the Federation for Catechesis with Hispanics (FCH)

And that brings us to what is the primary topic of this chapter and, in essence, of the entire book: the dimension of *being*. Above all else, catechetical leaders require formation that helps them to discover their vocation and to deepen their spirituality. In addition to acquiring deep knowledge of our faith and mastering the skills and methods for leading a faith-formation program, catechetical leaders need to be living and experiencing their Catholic faith—which means paying close attention to their spirituality. As a catechetical leader, you are not just the coordinator or director of a program. Rather, you are a witness to a living Person: Jesus Christ. As such, you are called to cultivate that relationship and to share that relationship with others. These actions—both the cultivation and the sharing of your relationship with Christ—make up your spirituality.

## The Spirituality of the Catechetical Minister

While every human being has a spirituality, each of our spiritualities is unique. Because of your vocation as a parish catechetical leader, you are called to ground your spiritual journey in several specific resources. These resources are identified and explored in the *Guide for Catechists* (1993), issued by the Vatican's Congregation for the Evangelization of Peoples. The *Guide* describes the spirituality of catechetical ministers. This unique spirituality is marked by the following six characteristics:

1. Openness to God—We recognize that God alone sustains us.
2. Openness to the church—We are not self-reliant.
3. Openness to the world—We seek God in all things and in all people.
4. Authenticity of life—We cannot give what we don't have.
5. Missionary zeal—We must be on fire with God's Word.
6. Devotion to Mary—We look to Mary and the saints for guidance.

Let's take a quick glance at each of these six aspects of the spirituality of catechetical ministers.

## Openness to God

Spirituality begins with the recognition that at our deepest level, we are incapable of sustaining ourselves and are therefore reliant upon a power outside ourselves. That power is God. For Christians, however, an openness to God is not just an intellectual assent to the existence of some nameless and faceless higher power. It is the act of embracing a loving relationship with a God of loving relationships. In Scripture, God reveals himself neither as some vague or nebulous higher power nor as the god of some smaller aspect of nature, such as the wind, rain, thunder, or fire. In revealing himself to Moses, God said, "I am the God of your father, the God of Abraham, the God of Isaac and the God of Jacob" (Exod. 3:6). In turn, Jesus said, "The Father and I are one" (John 10:30). Jesus is the face of God, and our God is a God who saves us. Our openness to God is nothing short of the admission of total reliance on a Person whom we recognize as the source of all life. The parish catechetical leader is one who deeply desires intimacy with God and is called to invite others to do the same. Openness to God is the desire to be transformed by this life-giving relationship and to invite others to this saving and sustaining transformation.

## Openness to the Church

In his book *The Road to Character* (Random House, 2015), David Brooks reminds us that "no person can achieve self-mastery on his or her own. Individual will, reason, compassion, and character are not strong enough to consistently defeat selfishness, pride, greed, and self-deception. Everybody needs redemptive assistance from outside—from family, friends, ancestors, rules, traditions, institutions, exemplars, and, for believers, God" (12). It is for this reason that followers of Christ are called to be spiritual *and* religious; to be one without the other is incomplete. Since our God is a God of relationships, he has chosen to communicate his redemptive will through his Son, Jesus Christ. Jesus, in turn, has entrusted his mission to his followers under the guidance of the Holy Spirit. As a catechetical leader, you are not self-reliant. Rather, you are called forth and sent on a mission in the name of Jesus Christ (and his church), through whom you find redemption. As you carry out this mission, you will be fed, supported, and nourished by the church. To be open to the church means to recognize and appreciate the relationship that was forged and formed in baptism when you became a member of the People of God, the church. As with any human relationship, this relationship with the church can sometimes involve tension and conflict. However, the healthy catechetical leader always remembers and honors the source of his or her redemptive grace, which comes from Jesus through his church by the power of the Holy Spirit.

## Openness to the World

Our God of relationships created the world and everything in it as a gift to his children. Our God of relationships continues to care for his world and everyone and everything in it. In fact, God loved the world so much that he sent his only Son to live among his children. God has not turned his back on the world but rather can be found reflected in it. As a catechetical leader, you are called to minister in the image of God, who delights in the world and does not run from it. Our call to be in relationship with God entails and necessitates our entering into a relationship with the world and all our fellow humans. Openness to the world means that we proclaim a gospel that takes flesh in the world, that seeks to recognize God already present in the world, and that embraces what is good in the world while calling that which falls short to rise up to its potential. As a catechetical leader, your mission is not to call people to retreat from the world but to enter into it more deeply in order to truly encounter God's people where they are. This is not to suggest that you should simply immerse yourself in the world and identify blindly with it. Rather, it means to encounter the world, engage it, and challenge it to be transformed in and through Christ so that it more clearly resembles the world that God intends.

## Authenticity of Life

Ultimately, spirituality should lead us to become the person that God wants us to be. It is a way of discovering our true self and our true potential. Unfortunately, we can find ourselves spending too much time and energy presenting "false" versions of ourselves to the world, as if trying on different outfits in hopes of finding something that looks good and feels right. Our God of relationships helps us to see ourselves as we truly are—flawed yet redeemed. Our God of relationships invites us to "put on Christ"—to live in the image of his only Son, who came as one who humbly serves others. By virtue of your baptism, you have "put on" Christ and have become a member of his body. As a catechetical leader, you are called to invite others to do the same. Catechetical leadership is not a hat that you put on and take off as you please but a way of life that draws others closer to Jesus. Only by knowing Jesus authentically, internalizing his message, and following the Catholic way of life that leads to him will you be able to lead others to him, too.

## Missionary Zeal

Recently, I was speaking with a pastor of a large suburban Catholic parish in the Archdiocese of Chicago. He was relating the results of a focus group conducted by his and other Catholic parishes to determine why so many Catholics in the area were choosing to attend a nearby evangelical church. He noted the usual things: the desire for better preaching, better music, and a more welcoming community. However, he was most interested in a reason that he saw coming up more than he had expected: many of the respondents in the focus group said that they were attracted by the level of energy in the evangelical community and saw that as something that was lacking in their Catholic parish.

The Acts of the Apostles tells us that three thousand people were attracted to the early church, not because they were "wowed" by healings or miracles or impressed by soaring rhetoric from the apostles. Rather, they could not resist the contagious joy and energy of the apostles, who were filled with the Holy Spirit—so filled, in fact, that people wondered if they were intoxicated! As I explain in my book *Under the Influence of Jesus: The Transforming Experience of Encountering Christ*,

> Somewhere along the way, unfortunately, we lost this robust and ebullient approach to proclaiming the gospel, as if the church had instituted some kind of "prohibition" against the inebriating influence of the Holy Spirit. . . . [T]he time has come for this prohibition to be lifted. The New Evangelization—a renewal and refocusing of the church's mission in the twenty-first century—is a clarion call for Christians all over the world to drink deeply of the Holy Spirit and begin living a transformed life under the influence of Jesus Christ.

As a catechetical leader, you serve in a very public role. It is imperative that what flows from you, above all else, is a zeal for God's Word—a desire to see the Good News spread like wildfire. Pope Francis reminded us that Christians must not be "sourpusses" (*Evangelii Gaudium*) but must exude joy above all else. Spirituality is the practice of paying attention to the smoldering embers in your soul and inviting the Holy Spirit to stoke the flames and set you on fire for Christ so that others will find the notion of discipleship irresistible.

## Devotion to Mary

We all have role models and mentors—people we look up to and seek to emulate. We don't try to become them but rather strive to integrate some of their attitudes and behaviors into our own personality. Catholics look to Mary and the saints for just this reason: they show us how to live as disciples of Christ. Mary was the first teacher of Jesus and the first disciple. She is, as Pope St. John Paul II said in *Catechesi Tradendae*, a "living catechism" and a "model for catechists." The spirituality of all the baptized is enriched by devotion to Mary, but, as a catechetical leader, your ministry can be especially enriched by devotion to the Blessed Mother and to all the saints who show us the way to the true light of the world, Jesus Christ.

In an issue of NCCL's *Catechetical Leader* magazine (May/June, 2009), Fr. Joseph Pellegrino points out that in artworks, Mary, the Mother of Jesus, is often holding up the child Jesus "for him to bless the world, to bless us." He goes on to note that "just as Mary was resolved to make God present in the world through her faith and obedience, as catechists, we are called to make God present to the world. We need to resolve to present Jesus, the Lord, to the world." Mary models four distinct ways you as a catechetical leader can present Christ to the world as she did.

| **Mary** | **The Parish Catechetical Leader** |
|---|---|
| Mary was surprised by the angel's news that she had been chosen by God to bear his only Son. Mary courageously said yes to this invitation. | You were no doubt surprised when you were invited to consider serving the Lord as a catechetical leader. Few of us, if any, dreamed about growing up and becoming a DRE! Mary's "fiat" can inspire you to accept God's will, even when you don't fully understand it. |

| | |
|---|---|
| As soon as Mary accepted God's will to become the mother of our Savior, she sprang into action, visiting her cousin Elizabeth, who was also with child. | Like Mary, you are called to spring into action as a catechetical leader to be present to others, especially your catechists and the parents of the children in your program. |
| Mary is depicted in Scripture as treasuring God's mysterious actions in the world and "ponder[ing] them in her heart" (Luke 2:19). | As a catechetical leader, you, too, are called to be contemplative and to sit with the mysteries of life, pondering God's presence and movement in your life and in the lives of others. |
| Mary was at the foot of the cross as Jesus suffered and died. | In your ministry, you will find yourself in the presence of people who are suffering. Like Mary, you can be fully present to others in their time of need. |

## Summary: Choose the Better Part

*"There is need of only one thing. Mary has chosen the better part, which will not be taken away from her."* (Luke 10:42)

In the Gospel of Luke, we read that Jesus visited the home of Martha and Mary. While he was there, Martha found herself busy with all the tasks of hospitality while her sister Mary sat at the feet of Jesus and listened to his teachings. When Martha complained about this to Jesus, he responded by scolding Martha for her anxiousness and assuring her that Mary had "chosen the better part" (Luke 10:42). In your ministry of catechetical leadership, you will find yourself responsible for many administrative tasks and will no doubt grow anxious and wonder where help is going to come from. During times like these, remember not to ignore "the better part"—the act of putting aside the *doing* and *knowing* for a time so that you can *be* in the presence of Jesus and dwell on his living word. *Being* in God's presence is the heart of spirituality. As a catechetical minister, your spirituality will be sustained by being open to and reliant on God; by being open to the guidance and nourishment of the church; by being open to the possibility of finding God in all things and in all people in this world; by remembering that your authentic self is flawed, yet redeemed; by inviting the Holy Spirit to reignite your passion for ministry continually; and by looking to Mary and the saints to show you "how it's done."

## For Reflection and Discussion

- The notion of *being* might sound like a luxury that a busy minister cannot afford when there is so much knowing and doing to be done. Why is *being* so important to the role of the catechetical leader? What dangers await the person who focuses on *knowing* and *doing* but ignores *being*?
- For a catechetical leader, what are the benefits of being open to God? Open to the Church? Open to the world? Authentic? Filled with missionary zeal? Devoted to Mary? Respond with your own words and thoughts.

## Growing as a Catechetical Leader

Of the three dimensions of spiritual formation—*being*, *knowing*, and *doing*—which do I most need to attend to? Which is my strength? How are all three interconnected?

Go to www.loyolapress.com/ECL to access the worksheet.

The Effective Catechetical Leader — NATIONAL CONFERENCE CATECHETICAL LEADERSHIP — LOYOLAPRESS.

### Assessing My Spiritual Wellness

Take a moment to assess your spiritual wellness by reflecting on each of the six characteristics of the spirituality of the catechetical minister. Write a few thoughts about what you can do to improve or sustain your spiritual wellness in each area.

| Spiritual Characteristics of the Catechetical Minister | Rate from 1 to 5, with 1 being the lowest (this is my weakness) and 5 being the highest (this is my strength). | What can I do to improve or sustain my spiritual wellness in this area? |
|---|---|---|
| **Openness to God** I recognize that God alone sustains me, and I turn to God to ask for his strength and grace in all that I do. | 1 2 3 4 5 | |
| **Openness to the Church** I recognize that I am called and sent by the church, and I seek its wisdom and guidance. | 1 2 3 4 5 | |
| **Openness to the World** I recognize God's grace and presence in the world, and I confidently strive to bring hope to the world. | 1 2 3 4 5 | |
| **Authenticity of Life** I have a living relationship with the Lord, and I sincerely believe and practice what I preach to others. | 1 2 3 4 5 | |
| **Missionary Zeal** I have a high level of energy and enthusiasm for my ministry, and I feel inspired to go forth and serve others. | 1 2 3 4 5 | |
| **Devotion to Mary and the Saints** I look to Mary and the saints for guidance and inspiration in my ministry. | 1 2 3 4 5 | |



**Called By Name:** Preparing Yourself for the Vocation of the Catechetical Leader — Chapter 4

## Suggested Action

The myth of our modern world is that the more we do, the better our lives will be. Actually, the opposite is true: the less we do, the more real, human, and "here" we become. Today, find a bench or a stoop in a pleasant spot and sit quietly on it for at least ten minutes. Practice going to this spot at least once a day just to pause and let your soul catch up with your body.

## For Further Consideration

To further explore the topic of this chapter, consider the following resources:

*The Catechist's Backpack: Spiritual Essentials for the Journey.* Joe Paprocki and Julianne Stanz (Chicago: Loyola Press, 2015).

*The Power of Pause: Becoming More by Doing Less.* Terry Hershey (Chicago: Loyola Press, 2009).

*Guide for Catechists.* (Congregation for the Evangelization of Peoples, 2017).

# 5

# Practicing the Art of Being: Spirituality and Spiritual Awareness

The average person today is not clamoring for a steady diet of doctrine, nor is it your role as a catechetical leader primarily to transmit doctrine. That's not to say that doctrine is unimportant. It is absolutely crucial to a full and mature faith. However, we don't lead with doctrine. We don't lead with moral pronouncements. Rather, we lead with the proclamation of a Person—Jesus Christ—and invite others into relationship with him. In other words, we lead with spirituality.

## That's the Spirit!

As a catechetical leader, you are called to be a spiritual leader: one who nourishes the spiritual life of God's people. The people you serve are not looking for you to be a theologian (although they want your theology to be sound) but rather a spiritual companion—someone who can help them to find God in their everyday lives and deepen their friendship with him.

In general, spirituality refers to how humans experience and nurture their relationship with God. Every human being has a spirituality. In the Christian spiritual tradition, a person relates to God in and through Jesus Christ. When we actively pursue it, Christian spirituality is a path to holiness.

While the spiritual lives of all Christians share certain characteristics, each person's spirituality is unique. It is influenced by his or her

- education
- formation
- gender
- geographical location
- age
- cultural/ethnic background

and so on. Thus, we can speak of spiritualities that are Celtic, Ignatian, Dominican, and Hispanic, just to name a few. By the same token, a person's spirituality is influenced by his or her vocation or state in life. A married person has a different spirituality than a celibate priest or nun. A single person's spiritual life expresses itself differently than that of a married person.

With that in mind, we can talk about the spirituality of catechetical ministers: all those who facilitate faith formation with children, youth, young adults, or adults in general. God has called you to a unique ministry, and therefore you have a unique spirituality. For you to tend to the spirituality of others, it is imperative that you begin by tending to your own spirituality.

## Are You Looking for More?

The spiritual life begins with this question: *Are you looking for more?* To be a spiritual person means to believe that there is more to life than meets the eye and to thirst for that "something more." Spiritual health is found through quenching that thirst by drinking from the right cup. Just as the body's immune system is strengthened by proper care (diet, exercise, stress management), our spiritual wellness relies on balance and harmony. Without that balance, we find ourselves settling for less instead of striving for more—evidence that our spirit needs healing.

Fortunately, we have a Divine Physician, Jesus Christ, who offers us a path to spiritual wellness.

Spiritual wellness enables us to experience "the more" that we seek. Unfortunately, many people today see Christianity less as a spiritual path and more as a code of ethics. While Christianity does indeed involve a moral code, the core of Jesus' Good News is an invitation to walk a spiritual path that leads to intimacy with our Creator. Simply put, Christian spirituality is the belief that God—the "more" that our heart desires—is accessible through Jesus Christ and his living word. As a catechetical leader, you are called to help the Church recover the spirituality of the Christian message, enabling followers of Jesus to experience the spiritual wellness that Jesus promises when he says, "Peace I leave with you; my peace I give to you" (John 14:27).

## Who's Feeding Whom?

It is common today to hear people talking about "feeding the soul." We even have books that claim to nourish the soul with "chicken soup"! Unfortunately, we have it backwards—we don't need to feed the soul; we need to let our souls feed us. Our souls are immortal and unchanging because they are the *imago Dei*—the image of God—who is immortal and unchanging. Our souls do not wither if we ignore them. Rather, *we* wither when we do not allow our soul—the imago Dei—to nurture us. Our goal, then, is not to feed and care for the soul but rather to allow our soul to feed and care for us.

How do we do this? We begin with a pause. In *The Power of Pause*, Terry Hershey tells the story of an American traveler on safari in Africa who had done good research and put together an itinerary and a timetable full of activities. He had even hired some local people to carry supplies as he traveled. For several days, he and his helpers awakened early and covered great distances at a frenzied pace. After several days, however, the helpers refused to get going one morning, opting instead to sit in the shade of a tree. When the traveler voiced his displeasure with them and demanded to know why they wouldn't move, a translator responded, "They're waiting for their souls to catch up with their bodies" (xix).

We need our souls to nurture and refresh us, and that begins when we pause to allow our souls to "catch up" with our bodies. We need to put aside *knowing* and *doing* and focus just on *being*. In *Beyond the Catechist's Toolbox: Catechesis That Not Only Informs but Also Transforms*, I note that in the kingdom of God, the primary form of expression is silence. Thomas Keating, a Trappist monk, tells us, "Silence is God's first language; everything else is a poor translation. In order to hear that language, we must learn to be still and to rest in God" (*Invitation to Love*). This stillness and silence—this spiritual pause—are not empty spaces but are, as Pope Benedict XVI explains, "a silence with content, not just the absence of speech and action." Silence for him is a positive stillness that restores us and helps us to "rediscover the one thing necessary" (*The Spirit of the Liturgy*). It "has the capacity to open a space in our inner being, a space in which God can dwell, which can ensure that His Word remains with us, and that love for Him is rooted in our minds and hearts, and animates our lives" (David Kerr, Catholic News Agency, March 7, 2012).

## Tapping into the Soul

In *Inner Compass: An Invitation to Ignatian Spirituality*, Margaret Silf tells about the time she attended a parish reception and noticed that, of all the goodies on the refreshment table, one large bowl of rice salad had remained untouched. She felt bad for the person who had prepared this rejected salad—until she realized it had gone untouched because it was missing a spoon! Silf goes on to explain that our spirituality is often like this: our soul is waiting to feed our deep hunger, but we lack a spoon. In other words, we lack the tools that will help us receive the soul's nourishment. As a catechetical leader, your job is to help people recognize their hunger and to provide them with the "utensils" they need to be nourished by the presence of God.

Throughout the history of the church, some very wise people have provided us with such utensils:

- John of the Cross
- Teresa of Avila
- Francis of Assisi
- Thérèse of Lisieux
- Brother Lawrence
- Augustine of Hippo
- Alphonsus Ligouri
- Catherine of Siena
- Benedict of Nursia

and many more. A very effective "delivery person" was St. Ignatius of Loyola, who designed tools not for monks in monasteries but for regular people in the secular world. The school of spirituality he founded—based on his work *The Spiritual Exercises*—provides exactly the diet and the exercise our spirit needs to stay healthy.

Ignatian spirituality is a good match for catechetical ministry because it is not focused on monastic living but rather on nurturing a friendship with Jesus while working to promote God's plan and action in the world. At its core, Ignatian spirituality concentrates on "finding God in all things," which is ultimately the goal of the catechetical ministry. Ignatius wrote *The Spiritual Exercises* based on his own experience of conversion and his desire to grow in intimacy with God and to discern God's will. Whether you are able to do the Spiritual Exercises of St. Ignatius, it can be helpful to you in your catechetical ministry to be aware of and to reflect on the themes of the Exercises. They are arranged into four "weeks"—understood not as seven-day cycles, but as stages on a journey to spiritual wellness.

- The first week of the Exercises invites us to reflect on our lives in light of the boundless love that God has for us. This week calls us to become more aware of our shortcomings (patterns of sin) and how they have been preventing us from attaining a deeper relationship with God. It invites us to approach the Lord, who always responds to us with mercy.

- The second week invites us to consider discipleship by focusing on the Person we are choosing to follow—Jesus Christ. By reflecting on the life, teachings, words, and actions of Jesus, we discern how we must change our lives to become disciples of Christ.
- The third week of the Exercises invites us to enter the Passion and death of Jesus in order to recognize the great gift of his selfless love—the total sacrifice of himself as the ultimate expression of God's love.
- Finally, in the fourth week, we are invited to reflect on the Resurrection of Jesus Christ and to walk with him as he leads us into the world to bring his love to others.

Ignatius teaches us that a healthy spirituality calls us to

- **reform** that which is ill-formed (tainted by sin);
- **conform** ourselves to the mind and heart of Jesus Christ;
- **confirm** our commitment to Christ, who gave himself to us; and
- **transform** our lives in the light of the risen Christ.

Throughout the Exercises, we are invited to meditate—to use our minds and imaginations to ponder the words and actions of Jesus Christ in the Gospel stories and to pay attention to the interior movements of our hearts, discerning where they might be leading us. St. Ignatius inspires us to develop a spirituality that is a true collaboration with God's action in the world and that leads us to practice spiritual discernment in decision making. He inspires us to find God in all things and to respond with generosity to God's abundant grace, living as a person for others.

## Another Utensil for Pausing

St. Ignatius developed a tool—a utensil—that enables busy laypeople to stay connected to their souls. This tool is known as the Daily Examen. The Examen is a process of prayerful reflection on the events of the day to recognize God's presence in them and to discern his will for us. Ignatius encouraged his followers to practice the Examen twice daily—once at noon and once at the end of the day. During each fifteen- to twenty-minute period, Ignatius encourages us to do the following.

- Become aware of God's presence and then look back on the events of the day with the help of the Holy Spirit.
- Review the day with gratitude, which is the foundation of our relationship with God. Walk through your day with the Lord, and focus on the day's gifts. Look at the work you did, the people you interacted with, and the experiences you had—and be thankful for them.
- Pay attention to your emotions, and ask the Spirit to help you discern what God is saying to you through them. Honestly identify some ways in which you fell short, and ask God for his mercy.
- Focus on one feature of the day and pray from it, asking the Holy Spirit to help you discern God's will for you.
- Look forward to the rest of the day or to tomorrow, asking God for the grace you need to be a true disciple of Christ.

St. Ignatius encourages us to talk to Jesus like a friend. He suggests that we end our Daily Examen in conversation with Jesus, asking—in a spirit of gratitude—for his forgiveness, his guidance, and his grace. Finally, Ignatius suggests that we conclude the Daily Examen by praying the Lord's Prayer.

## A More Formal Approach to Your Soul

Spiritual direction was once largely reserved for the "spiritual elite"—priests and religious. Today, however, many laypeople and lay ministers—including catechetical leaders such as yourself—are seeking the counsel of a spiritual director. What *is* spiritual direction, you ask? According to William Barry, SJ, spiritual direction is "help given by one Christian to another which enables that person to pay attention to God's personal communication to him or her, to respond to this personally communicating God, to grow in intimacy with this God, and to live out the consequences of the relationship" (*The Practice of Spiritual Direction*). Spiritual direction is not therapy. Nor is it some type of rigorous regimen of monastic prayer practices or some esoteric experience. It is simply a matter of talking with a companion about your life experiences with an eye to finding God's grace in the midst of them. We'll revisit the notion of spiritual direction in more depth in chapter 9.

## The Eucharist, the Sacrament of Reconciliation, and Devotions

At the heart of any Catholic's spiritual life is the Eucharist, the source and summit of the Christian life. Spiritually, we are always hungry and in need of nourishment. Nothing satisfies the hungry heart like the "gift of finest wheat" that is the Eucharist. God alone is our source of fulfillment: not our looks, money, possessions, status, friends, family, geographical location, economic status, popularity, power, or abilities. God alone.

Some clubs or groups have a symbol that represents who they are: a flag, an emblem, a secret handshake, or a uniform. For Catholics, the Eucharist—something we do, something we celebrate—is the ultimate expression of who we are: the Body of Christ. The message of the Eucharist is very clear. At our deepest level, we are incapable of sustaining ourselves. We rely on the Lord. For catechetical leaders, there is no better way to find sustenance and spiritual nourishment than through the Eucharist, including spending time before the Blessed Sacrament in prayerful adoration.

Another important avenue of grace for the catechetical leader is the sacrament of reconciliation. Our Catholic faith is not about picking ourselves up by our bootstraps when we have fallen. Rather, it is about relying totally on the grace and mercy of God to lift us up. In the sacrament of reconciliation, we find the grace of forgiveness that we need to overcome our human frailties. It is particularly beneficial to know in your heart and soul that your relationship with God and the Church is in a healthy state. And, of course, the peace and serenity of conscience, the spiritual consolation, and the increase of spiritual strength found in the sacrament of reconciliation are beneficial to any pastoral minister.

Finally, many catechetical leaders find great spiritual nourishment in regular reading of and praying with Scripture (especially Lectio Divina) and in devotional practices, particularly the rosary.

## Spirituality Is Ultimately about Being for Others

In his opening comments to the World Meeting of Families in Philadelphia in 2016, Bishop Robert Barron spoke about living as the *imago Dei*—as the image of God. He remarked that the divine image "is not some little special privilege that we hang on to for our own spiritual benefit. Rather, as in the great parable of the talents, the image of God is for the world. We must think of ourselves as representatives of God, bringing His power, His wisdom, His heart, His mind to the world. The image of God is a mission and a responsibility."

Bishop Barron's words were directed at families, but they are applicable to the role of catechetical leader as well. Paying attention to your own spiritual wellness is ultimately a prerequisite to paying attention to the spiritual wellness of others. And it all begins by pausing and getting in touch with your soul and allowing yourself to fall in love with God. In the words of Pedro Arrupe, Superior General of the Jesuits from 1965 to 1983, "What you are in love with, what seizes your imagination, will affect everything. It will decide what will get you out of bed in the morning, what you will do with your evenings, how you will spend your weekends, what you read, who you know, what breaks your heart, and what amazes you with joy and gratitude. Fall in love, stay in love and it will decide everything."

May your imagination be seized with a love of God that propels you out of bed each morning to share that love with others.

## Summary: You Have Heard It Said

*You have heard that it was said, "An eye for an eye and a tooth for a tooth." But I say to you, do not resist an evildoer. But if anyone strikes you on the right cheek, turn the other also; and if anyone wants to sue you and take your coat, give your cloak as well; and if anyone forces you to go one mile, go also the second mile. Give to everyone who begs from you, and do not refuse anyone who wants to borrow from you.*
(Matt. 5:38–42)

Jesus has a vision for an alternate reality—the kingdom of God—a state of being in which God's will reigns. Our souls are designed to live in this reality, and the role of spirituality is to let our souls nourish us so that we can live as true disciples of Christ. As a catechetical leader, you are called to be a spiritual leader, not a theologian. Your task is to seek "the more" of the kingdom of God by paying attention to your own spiritual wellness so that you can help others do the same. St. Ignatius of Loyola provides us with many "utensils" for serving up healthy portions of spiritual nutrition, particularly his *Spiritual Exercises* and the Daily Examen. For Catholics, the heart of spiritual wellness and our greatest source of nourishment is the Eucharist.

Other sources of spiritual nourishment, including the sacrament of reconciliation and devotions such as praying the rosary, can help sustain you as well.

## For Reflection and Discussion

- "We don't need to feed our souls; we need to let our souls feed us." What does this mean to you?
- What is your experience and familiarity with Ignatian spirituality, especially the *Spiritual Exercises* and the Daily Examen?

## Growing as a Catechetical Leader

Our spiritual lives rely on having good "utensils" that allow our soul to feed us with the food we crave. What "utensils" are you presently using to receive the nourishment of your soul? What "utensils" do you need to acquire?

Go to www.loyolapress.com/ECL to access the worksheet.

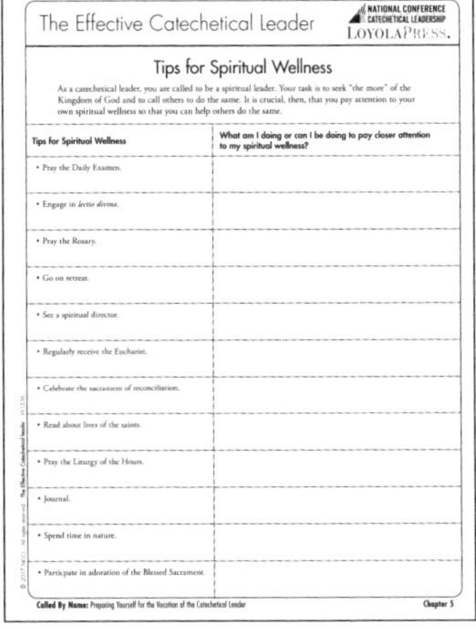

The Effective Catechetical Leader

NATIONAL CONFERENCE CATECHETICAL LEADERSHIP
LOYOLAPRESS.

Tips for Spiritual Wellness

As a catechetical leader, you are called to be a spiritual leader. Your task is to seek "the more" of the Kingdom of God and to call others to do the same. It is crucial, then, that you pay attention to your own spiritual wellness so that you can help others do the same.

| Tips for Spiritual Wellness | What am I doing or can I be doing to pay closer attention to my spiritual wellness? |
|---|---|
| • Pray the Daily Examen. | |
| • Engage in *lectio divina*. | |
| • Pray the Rosary. | |
| • Go on retreat. | |
| • See a spiritual director. | |
| • Regularly receive the Eucharist. | |
| • Celebrate the sacrament of reconciliation. | |
| • Read about lives of the saints. | |
| • Pray the Liturgy of the Hours. | |
| • Journal. | |
| • Spend time in nature. | |
| • Participate in adoration of the Blessed Sacrament. | |

**Called By Name:** Preparing Yourself for the Vocation of the Catechetical Leader — **Chapter 5**

## Suggested Action

St. Ignatius considered the Daily Examen to be nonnegotiable for his followers, especially for those who were unable to celebrate the Eucharist regularly because of their location in the world. The Daily Examen offers you a valuable method for maintaining your spiritual wellness as a catechetical leader. Set aside fifteen to twenty minutes to practice the Examen—once at midday and once in the evening—as regularly as possible.

## For Further Consideration

To further explore the topic of this chapter, consider the following resources:

*Open Mind, Open Heart.* Thomas Keating (New York: Continuum Publishing, 1986, 1992).

*Breathing under Water: Spirituality and the Twelve Steps.* Richard Rohr (Cincinnati, OH: St. Anthony Messenger Press, 2011).

*Inner Compass: An Invitation to Ignatian Spirituality.* Margaret Silf (Chicago: Loyola Press, 1999).

*And Now I See: A Theology of Transformation.* Bishop Robert Barron (New York: Crossroad Publishing, 1998).

*A Simple Life-Changing Prayer: Discovering the Power of St. Ignatius Loyola's Examen.* Jim Manney (Chicago: Loyola Press, 2011).

*God Finds Us: An Experience of the Spiritual Exercises of St. Ignatius Loyola.* Jim Manney (Chicago: Loyola Press, 2013).

# 6
# No Lone Rangers Need Apply: Lay Ecclesial Ministry

Have you ever noticed that many heroes in popular culture are loners? These heroes save the day, but they tend to do it all by themselves. Think of Batman, Superman, Iron Man, Wolverine, and (for those of us who are a little older) the Lone Ranger. Our heroes tend to be rugged individuals who engage in alliances or affiliations with others only reluctantly. A good example of this is Han Solo of *Star Wars* fame. While he does have his companion, Chewbacca, Han Solo resists the company, assistance, and especially the authority of others. He embodies the myth of the rugged individual who prefers to save the universe on his own. Even his name embodies the myth of individualism: *Solo*!

## The Myth of the Rugged Individualist

Rugged individualism is one of the most pervasive values in American culture. We value independence. Success, in our culture, tends to be attributed primarily to the hard work and perseverance of the individual. We love to think we can pull ourselves up by our bootstraps. Scripture, however, reminds us that to be a follower of Jesus is the opposite of being a rugged individualist; it is to be a member of a community of faith. Jesus himself was not a rugged individualist. While he may have spent forty days in solitude in the desert, the first thing he did upon emerging from that experience was to assemble a team—his twelve apostles—with whom he spent the next three years of his life.

## God Calls a People

Even in the Old Testament, while God did indeed call individuals to specific roles, he primarily called a people. In the New Testament, St. Paul reminds us that although we each have unique individual talents and gifts, it is the One Holy Spirit who holds us together as one Body and directs us to bring our talents to the service of the community. In the Gospel of John, Jesus performs his first miracle—changing water to wine—at a wedding feast in Cana. Nothing says community and togetherness like a wedding feast. Jesus does not appear out of nowhere to perform this miracle. He does not swoop in on a spider web or fly in with a flapping cape or arrive in his "Jesus mobile." He is in Cana as part of a community. He is there with his mother and with his disciples. It is within this tight-knit community celebration that Jesus reveals his glory.

## Prisca and Aquila

As followers of Jesus, we are called to participate in a community of faith—the church. For Catholics, faith is not so much a "me-and-God" experience as it is a "we-and-God" experience. (More about that in chapter 9.) As a catechetical leader, you are called not only to be a part of a community of faith but also to share in a special relationship with the successors of the apostles, the bishops. While many people serve in ministerial roles as lectors, extraordinary ministers of Holy Communion, catechists, and choir members, you have ventured into the unique role of *lay ecclesial minister*.

While this title was coined only recently, the reality of laypeople assisting the apostles and their successors in the ministry of building up the church can be traced to the very beginnings of Christianity. In the New Testament, for example, a married couple by the names of Prisca and Aquila are mentioned no fewer than six times as coworkers of the apostle Paul (Acts 18:2–3, 18, 26; Rom. 16:4; 1 Cor. 16:19; 2 Tim. 4:19). Prisca and Aquila were tentmakers, missionaries, and coworkers of St. Paul, a fellow tentmaker whom they met in Corinth. They worked together in the tent-making business for a while but eventually became coworkers in the vineyard of Christ as they teamed up to proclaim the gospel of Jesus Christ to the first-century world. Even as Paul continued in his missionary journeys, he maintained a connection with Prisca and Aquila. They continued the ministry that Paul invited them into and did so with the full recognition that they were sharing in Paul's work. A decade and a half after they met in Corinth, Paul mentioned Prisca and Aquila in the letter he wrote (Romans) while in prison in Rome. Even in the days leading up to his death in Rome, Paul affirms his connection with his coworkers Prisca and Aquila.

## How Did We Get Here?

In modern-day parlance, Prisca and Aquila were lay ecclesial ministers, a term approved by the United States Conference of Catholic Bishops and used in the document *Co-Workers in the Vineyard of the Lord* (2005) to refer to laypeople who serve the Church in specific roles but who are not ordained. We'll learn more about those roles shortly. In the meantime, let's look at how lay ecclesial ministry has evolved over the centuries. The following overview has been adapted from James Campbell's *Serving the Catechetical Mission of the Church*.

- **AD 33–125** The apostles and other disciples orally proclaimed the Good News of Jesus in the synagogues, telling stories and acting out scenes we now find in the Gospels. Eventually, Church teaching took on a written form as Paul and others proclaimed the Word in the Letters and Gospels.

- **125–300** The early church, facing a world that was hostile to Christian values, emphasized a personal relationship that conformed one to Christ. The central model for catechesis was the catechumenate—a process of initiation into the Christian way of life—and the bishop was the primary catechetical figure.
- **300–600** When Constantine made Christianity the official religion of the Roman Empire, great numbers of people became Christian. Although the catechumenate remained the primary model of catechesis and the bishop remained in a central catechetical role, the introduction of infant baptism placed a responsibility on parents to catechize their children in the home.
- **600–1100** As the Roman Empire and civilization collapsed in the "Dark Ages," monasteries provided order and stability while the catechumenate fell out of practice. Instead, entire populations of people were converted and instructed through preaching by the clergy. Meanwhile, parents were expected to instruct their children in the Apostles' Creed and the Lord's Prayer.
- **1100–1500** As civilization began to rebuild and the Catholic Church established the first universities, a way of thought known as scholasticism became the primary influence on pastors. Preaching and instruction focused less on the story of salvation and more on abstract theology and logical thought. Because most people on the European continent were born into communities shaped entirely by the Catholic faith, there was little need for systematic catechesis. Parents continued to instruct their children in the Creed, Catholic prayers, and other basic articles of the faith as well as devotions.
- **1500–1900** The invention of the printing press revolutionized catechesis as Bibles and catechetical materials could now be mass-produced. In response to the Protestant Reformation, the Council of Trent inspired the first universal catechism, and an

emphasis was placed on high-quality catechetical materials—local catechisms—that parish priests could use to faithfully teach the Catholic faith.

- **1840–1960** As immigrants flooded to the shores of the United States in the early 1800s and found a public-school system controlled by Protestants, the American church responded by creating the Catholic school system and formulated the *Baltimore Catechism*, which focused on the memorization of questions and answers centered on doctrinal formulas. Religious orders, primarily religious women, formed the "army" of catechists who oversaw this catechetical instruction in schools and CCD (Confraternity of Christian Doctrine) programs while the family continued to form children in prayer and devotions.
- **1960–Present Day** While parents continued to rely on the parish school or religious-education program to form their children in faith, the role of family and society changed radically beginning in the 1960s, resulting in less faith formation in the home. Meanwhile, as the number of priests and religious sharply declined, the number of laypeople in ministry exploded. Likewise, as enrollment in Catholic schools steadily decreased, the size of parish religious-education programs steadily increased—and, along with that development came a demand for professionally trained catechetical leaders. Today this role is filled primarily by lay ecclesial ministers.

## Responding to New Realities

Today catechetical programs continue to try to respond to new realities in society and especially in the family. At the forefront of this movement are lay ecclesial ministers who serve as catechetical leaders. According to the Center for Applied Research in the Apostolate (CARA, Research Review: "Lay Ecclesial Ministers in the United

States," February 2015), between 1990 and 2010 the number of priests in the United States declined from 52,000 to 40,000; the number of sisters from 103,000 to 58,000; and the number of brothers from 7,000 to 5,000. During that same period, the number of lay ecclesial ministers rose from 22,000 to nearly 40,000. Here are some other pertinent bits of information about this army of ministers that you now belong to.

- Eighty percent are women.
- The median age is 55, and only 15 percent are under 40.
- Eighty-nine percent consider their ministry a vocation, not just a job.
- About half work 40 hours on average per week.
- Forty-six percent have a graduate or professional degree.
- Eighty-eight percent are white; 9 percent are Hispanic; fewer than 2 percent are African American; fewer than 2 percent are Asian; and fewer than one percent are Native American.
- More than 4 in 10 serve in catechetical leadership.

The role of the lay ecclesial minister is characterized by the following four characteristics:

- **Authorization.** The lay ecclesial minister is authorized by the bishop or some other member of the church hierarchy to serve publicly in the local church. Such authorization takes the form of certification (acknowledgment that an individual has achieved required levels of competence), appointment (assignment or commissioning to a specific position), and a public announcement of the appointment (often including a term of office) to the community he or she will serve. Just as when you take solace knowing that a doctor or lawyer has the proper credentials from a trusted source, it is good for the people of

God to know that their lay ecclesial ministers are properly credentialed and authorized by the bishop.

- **Leadership.** The lay ecclesial minister is called to serve in a particular area of ministry. Common roles assumed by lay ecclesial ministers in parish life include pastoral associates, parish catechetical leaders, youth ministers, school principals, and directors of liturgy or pastoral music. In addition, lay ecclesial ministers beyond parish life serve as pastoral care ministers in hospitals and health-care settings, as campus ministers, and as pastoral ministers in prisons and airports.

- **Close mutual collaboration.** The lay ecclesial minister is called to collaborate closely with (and be accountable to) the bishops, priests, and deacons in his or her diocese and parish. Lay ecclesial ministers are not replacements for the ordained, nor are they in competition with them. The role of the lay ecclesial minister is distinct from, yet complementary to, the role of the ordained.
- **Preparation and formation.** Lay ecclesial ministers are required to have sufficient preparation and formation for the specific role assigned to them. Canon law reminds us that "lay persons who devote themselves permanently or temporarily to some special service of the Church are obliged to acquire the appropriate

formation which is required to fulfill their function properly" (231). This formation focuses on development in four key areas: human qualities, spirituality, knowledge in theological and pastoral studies, and intellectual skills. Such formation is not designed to create a new clerical state or to foster a sense of elitism but rather to ensure that God's people are being served by people who themselves are fully prepared to serve effectively in their role. As a parish catechetical leader, you will be the face of the Church to many people in a variety of circumstances. Preparation and formation ensure that you will represent the church faithfully.

## Let's Build Something Together

The heart of lay ecclesial ministry is collaboration—which, truth be told, can be a scary word. As leadership expert Emmanuel Gobillot explains in his book *Disciplined Collaboration*, the idea of collaborating with others raises fears about the following:

- Loss of personal value—If I share what I know with others, do I become expendable?
- Loss of quality—Will quality suffer because I'll be required to compromise?
- Loss of momentum—If I have to work with others, won't things take longer than if I did them myself?
- Loss of control—Does collaboration mean that I'll lose control of certain aspects of my role?

These are all very real fears, and yet, as a lay ecclesial minister, you are being called to a generous and mutual collaboration—not only with fellow lay ecclesial ministers but also with bishops, priests, deacons, and other members of the Body of Christ in the church.

So, what is the key to effective collaboration? According to Gobillot, collaboration will be successful if and only if it adequately addresses these four fears.

| **To address the fear of the loss of . . .** | **The collaborator must . . .** |
|---|---|
| Personal value | Recognize and articulate the skills, qualities, and characteristics—not just the knowledge—that make him or her of great value to the group |
| Quality | Promote and articulate a sense of purpose that resonates and energizes other members of the group and strengthens bonds with them. |
| Momentum | Articulate a process and foster dialogue that builds momentum and brings separate elements together to achieve a desired outcome |
| Control | Let go of overall control while still being "in charge" of specific tasks |

By now, it should be dawning on you that true collaboration requires much more than just "being nice" to one another. It requires particular skills and a particular methodology.

Ultimately, any group of collaborators is working together to arrive at the knowledge and strategies needed to achieve a goal. But just how does a group of individuals come to know—or know how to do—*anything* together? The late Jesuit philosopher and theologian Bernard Lonergan outlined four imperatives for successful collaboration.

1. **Be attentive.** The first step in knowing together is to observe, to recognize, and to reflect on that which we are observing. For the lay ecclesial minister, this means listening to everyone's voice.

2. **Be intelligent.** The next step in knowing together is to probe, to question, to research, and to seek understanding and clarity on various viewpoints. For the lay ecclesial minister, this means asking the questions that need to be asked to gather necessary information for a group to move forward.
3. **Be reasonable.** The third step in knowing together is to make connections, to evaluate various approaches and viewpoints, and to make judgments. For the lay ecclesial minister, this means making connections wherever and whenever appropriate and possible and coming to a decision based on the evidence and viewpoints that have been presented.
4. **Be responsible.** The final step in knowing together is making a commitment to act and then be accountable for the actions taken. For the lay ecclesial minister, this means committing to a course of action that is truly the work of collaboration and then standing by the action when it is evaluated later and accepting the feedback as an opportunity to learn and grow—at which point the process begins all over again.

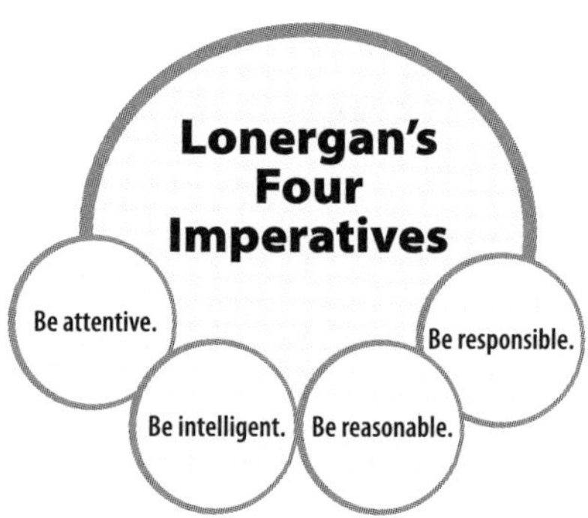


Lonergan's four imperatives—be attentive, be intelligent, be reasonable, and be responsible—while designed with the attainment of individual knowledge in mind, are equally applicable to collaboration. For Catholics, collaboration is not primarily a technique for "getting things done" but an expression of who we are: the Body of Christ. In *Sharing Wisdom*, Mary Benet McKinney, O.S.B., explains that "no one has all the wisdom; everyone has a different piece; everyone has some of the wisdom." According to McKinney, collaboration does indeed ask more of us because it is not a model for management but a process of becoming church.

So what qualities are needed for a lay ecclesial minister to excel at collaboration? According to Dan Ebener (*Servant Leadership Models for Your Parish*), the following are key:

- **Respect** for others
- **Openness** to various viewpoints and ideas
- **Fairness** in providing equitable time for differing viewpoints
- **Willingness to listen** to the needs of others
- **Privacy** and respect for confidentiality
- **Presence** to others and attention to their viewpoints
- **Commitment** to achieving the desired outcome of the group

## All That Jazz

The essence of jazz is improvisation by one group member in response to improvisation by another. The musical voices converse and blend to create something new and unique. For a jazz collaboration to be successful, the members of the ensemble must be egalitarian; they must be good listeners; they must be interactive and responsive; and they must be willing to change course "on the fly."

In many ways, the skills that jazz musicians rely on to achieve this high level of collaboration apply to collaboration in ministry. Consider the following list of skills created by jazz radio show host Scott McDowell, titled "What Jazz Soloists Know About Creative Collaboration." For each skill McDowell identifies, I've added a thought or two about its connection to collaboration in ministry.

- **Constant practice.** By constantly practicing, jazz musicians can intuit what their fellow musicians are up to. As a lay ecclesial minister, every exchange with fellow ministers is an opportunity to develop the ability to intuit where your fellow ministers are coming from.
- **Listening.** A jazz musician learns to pay attention to his or her fellow musicians, picking up clues from body language and tone. As a lay ecclesial minister, you also must pay close attention to what fellow ministers are saying rather than just think of how you will respond.
- **Innovation.** Jazz musicians learn to develop new approaches rather than rely on the same old formulas and patterns. As a lay ecclesial minister, you will learn to let go of "the way you've always done things" to improvise—to address each situation with a fresh approach.
- **Spurring others into action.** Jazz musicians learn to play notes that either support or provoke fellow band members or soloists, encouraging them to sharpen their own ideas and thus bringing out the best in them. As a lay ecclesial minister, one of the most effective ways to collaborate is to focus on bringing out the best in those around you and, as a jazz musician might say, "transfer energy" to them.
- **Failing admirably.** Because they rely so heavily on innovation, jazz musicians learn to accept missteps as part of the process that leads to greatness. True collaboration in ministry can be fostered by a willingness to admit and embrace mistakes—your own and those of others—as a natural part of the process.

In the end, a collaborator is someone who operates with more of a "we" focus than a "me" focus; someone who is appreciative of the gifts others bring to the group; someone who is trusting and trustworthy, who builds relationships, and who is more of a diplomat than a warrior. As a lay ecclesial minister, collaboration is one of your primary responsibilities as well as one of your most important tools. For the lay ecclesial minister, true collaboration is not so much a strategy for efficiently achieving a task but an end itself—an expression and an experience of faith. It therefore seems fitting to end this chapter with the words used by the U.S. bishops to conclude their document *Co-Workers in the Vineyard of the Lord*:

> We are blessed indeed to have such gifted and generous co-workers in the vineyard of the Lord to which we have all been called. Let us continue to work together as a "community of people united in Christ and guided by the Holy Spirit in [our] pilgrimage toward the Father's kingdom, bearers of a message for all humanity."

## Summary: God Causes All Things to Work Together

*We know that all things work together for good for those who love God, who are called according to his purpose.* (Rom. 8:28)

Sometimes it may seem easier and more appealing to do things by yourself. Going solo is, after all, the "American way." As a member of the Body of Christ and as a lay ecclesial minister, however, you are called to work together—to collaborate—with other key members of the Church to further the kingdom of God. Lay ecclesial ministry is new in some ways and yet has ancient roots in our Church. The key characteristics of serving as a lay ecclesial minister are that you have been authorized by church leadership, you have assumed a specific leadership role in ministry, you collaborate generously with peers and superiors, and you are committed to ongoing formation. Bernard Lonergan, SJ, provides us with a sound strategy for effective collaboration: be attentive, be intelligent, be reasonable, and be responsible.

## For Reflection and Discussion

- How is serving as a lay ecclesial minister the antithesis of the American myth of the rugged individualist?
- What have been your experiences of collaboration? When they have been successful, what made them so? What specific gifts do you bring to the process of collaboration?

## Growing as a Catechetical Leader

Collaboration is at the heart of serving effectively as a lay ecclesial minister. Who are the key people you are called to collaborate with? What about this collaboration is positive? What obstacles does the collaboration face?

Go to www.loyolapress.com/ECL to access the worksheet.

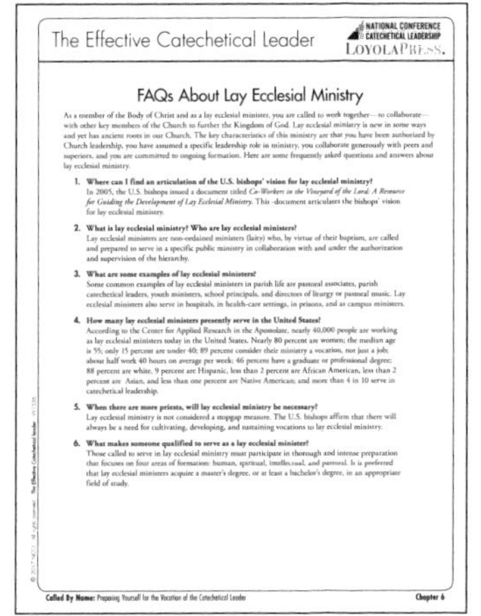

The Effective Catechetical Leader

NATIONAL CONFERENCE CATECHETICAL LEADERSHIP
LOYOLAPRESS.

FAQs About Lay Ecclesial Ministry

As a member of the Body of Christ and as a lay ecclesial minister, you are called to work together—to collaborate—with other key members of the Church to further the Kingdom of God. Lay ecclesial ministry is new in some ways and yet has ancient roots in our Church. The key characteristics of this ministry are that you have been authorized by Church leadership, you have assumed a specific leadership role in ministry, you collaborate generously with peers and superiors, and you are committed to ongoing formation. Here are some frequently asked questions and answers about lay ecclesial ministry.

1. **Where can I find an articulation of the U.S. bishops' vision for lay ecclesial ministry?**
   In 2005, the U.S. bishops issued a document titled *Co-Workers in the Vineyard of the Lord: A Resource for Guiding the Development of Lay Ecclesial Ministry.* This -document articulates the bishops' vision for lay ecclesial ministry.
2. **What is lay ecclesial ministry? Who are lay ecclesial ministers?**
   Lay ecclesial ministers are non-ordained ministers (laity) who, by virtue of their baptism, are called and prepared to serve in a specific public ministry in collaboration with and under the authorization and supervision of the hierarchy.
3. **What are some examples of lay ecclesial ministers?**
   Some common examples of lay ecclesial ministers in parish life are pastoral associates, parish catechetical leaders, youth ministers, school principals, and directors of liturgy or pastoral music. Lay ecclesial ministers also serve in hospitals, in health-care settings, in prisons, and as campus ministers.
4. **How many lay ecclesial ministers presently serve in the United States?**
   According to the Center for Applied Research in the Apostolate, nearly 40,000 people are working as lay ecclesial ministers today in the United States. Nearly 80 percent are women; the median age is 55; only 15 percent are under 40; 89 percent consider their ministry a vocation, not just a job; about half work 40 hours on average per week; 46 percent have a graduate or professional degree; 88 percent are white, 9 percent are Hispanic, less than 2 percent are African American, less than 2 percent are Asian, and less than one percent are Native American; and more than 4 in 10 serve in catechetical leadership.
5. **When there are more priests, will lay ecclesial ministry be necessary?**
   Lay ecclesial ministry is not considered a stopgap measure. The U.S. bishops affirm that there will always be a need for cultivating, developing, and sustaining vocations to lay ecclesial ministry.
6. **What makes someone qualified to serve as a lay ecclesial minister?**
   Those called to serve in lay ecclesial ministry must participate in thorough and intense preparation that focuses on four areas of formation: human, spiritual, intellectual, and pastoral. It is preferred that lay ecclesial ministers acquire a master's degree, or at least a bachelor's degree, in an appropriate field of study.

**Called By Name:** Preparing Yourself for the Vocation of the Catechetical Leader — **Chapter 6**

## Suggested Action

Bernard Lonergan, SJ, offers four imperatives for successful collaboration: be attentive, be intelligent, be reasonable, and be responsible. Apply these four imperatives to an experience of collaboration in which you are presently engaged. How can each imperative assist you in being a more effective collaborator?

## For Further Consideration

To further explore the topic of this chapter, consider the following resources:

*Co-Workers in the Vineyard of the Lord: A Resource for Guiding the Development of Lay Ecclesial Ministry.* USCCB (Washington, D.C., 2006).

*Sharing Wisdom: A Process for Group Decision Making.* Mary Benet McKinney, O.S.B. (Allen, TX: Tabor Publishing, 1987).

*Lay Ecclesial Ministry: Pathways toward the Future* edited by Zeni Fox (Lanham, MD: Rowman & Littlefield Publishers, 2010).

*Servant Leadership Models for Your Parish* Dan R. Ebener (Mahwah, NJ: Paulist Press, 2010).

# 7

# Two Sides of the Same Coin: A Covenant Relationship

In one of my favorite movies, *Young Frankenstein*, Teri Garr plays the role of Inga, Dr. Frankenstein's assistant. She uses an exaggerated German accent that results in her hilariously pronouncing the phrase *the feeling is mutual* as "the feeling is moochal." That has no significant bearing on this chapter other than the fact that I can't hear, see, or say the word *mutual* without hearing it pronounced as Inga did! All of that to say that a key word in this chapter is *mutuality*.

## Mutuality

All healthy relationships rely on some degree of mutuality. In other words, both parties recognize and share a common goal and commit to contributing equitably toward the achievement of that goal. The arrangement is not a quid pro quo agreement; it goes far beyond a this-for-that exchange. Instead of a mathematical trade, there is a rich and selfless sharing—a reciprocity that enables each partner to thrive and enjoy the benefits of the relationship without being depleted by constant giving and no receiving.

In Scripture, especially the Old Testament, this concept of mutuality is expressed in the word *covenant*. In the ancient Near East, people entered covenants, which spelled out rights and responsibilities, to ensure that they could work together in an effective manner. For the Israelites, the central covenant was the sacred relationship between God and the people of Israel. In this covenant, initiated by God, the people of Israel had certain obligations placed on them—namely, the Torah, which includes the Ten Commandments—in return for the promise of God's never-ending presence and love. Other covenants of the time were between equals, but the covenant between God and the Israelites was not. This made it all the more sacred to them. Their God was great beyond comprehension but was willing to meet them halfway, to call them again and again into his constant presence.

## A Sacred Relationship

In your role as a lay ecclesial minister, it can be useful to think of your relationship with the church as a covenant. While at times the relationship looks like a business contract, it is much more than that; it is a sacred relationship. As a lay ecclesial minister, you are in a symbiotic relationship with the church. Like any other relationship, this one can be very complex. At its heart, however, is a quality of mutuality. Both you and the church have rights and responsibilities: you "owe" the church something, while the church, as your employer, "owes" you something as well. You occupy two sides of the same coin.

In this chapter, we will explore both sides of the coin, keeping in mind that this relationship does not involve adversaries but rather members of the same team—the Body of Christ—who seek the same end: the proclamation of the Good News to all the world! To identify and articulate these rights and duties is a way to promote the professionalism and ensure the competence of lay ecclesial ministers and, thus, the excellence of Catholic parishes.

## What You Owe the Church

### Highly Competent Pastoral Ministry According to Your Gifts and Specific Role Description

The church has hired you for a specific reason: to provide service as a lay ecclesial minister with particular responsibilities. It is important for both parties that these responsibilities be clearly defined. The role of parish catechetical leaders comes in a variety of shapes and sizes and varies from parish to parish and diocese to diocese. Some serve as directors of religious education and faith formation, possess a graduate degree in theology or pastoral studies, and are responsible for all aspects of faith formation in the parish, from "womb to tomb." Others are hired as coordinators of religious education and faith formation. These ministers may have certification or advanced certification as a catechist rather than a graduate degree, and they may or may not assume responsibility for the children's faith-formation program. Some roles are full-time, others are part-time, and still others are volunteer positions. Whatever your title or salary (or lack thereof!), you owe it to the church to "deliver" on your promise to carry out your ministerial responsibilities to the best of your ability, according to the agreed-upon scope of your role.

### Faithfulness to Church Teaching and Respect for Church Authority

Remember what we said about not being a lone ranger. You owe it to the Church to faithfully transmit the teachings of Jesus and the apostles as they have been handed on to you. While there may be times that you find yourself struggling with a particular Church teaching or practice, it is your responsibility to pray for the grace needed to reflect more deeply on that particular issue, come to a better understanding of what the Church teaches and why, and present that teaching faithfully to parishioners. Whether you confidentially share your own opinions in private settings with trusted friends or family members is up to you. But in public settings, you owe it to the Church to present its teachings faithfully and to speak about Church authority and those in authority with respect.

## Commitment to Ongoing Formation

In the catechetical ministry, we preach that faith formation is a lifelong endeavor. We never stop growing in faith because God is infinite and we are called to enter ever more deeply into God's mystery. As a catechetical minister, you are called to practice what you preach, striving to participate in ongoing formation: human, spiritual, intellectual, and pastoral. Ongoing formation is one of the ways that you remain sharp and stay abreast of current issues, trends, and approaches in catechetical ministry. In *The 7 Habits of Highly Effective People*, Stephen Covey identifies "sharpening the saw"—setting aside time for renewal, growth, and self-improvement—as the seventh habit. You owe it to the Church to continue to "sharpen your saw" as a catechetical leader so that you can effectively call others to grow in their faith and discipleship.

## Honesty, Integrity, Virtue, and Accountability

As noted earlier, you will be the face of the church for many people and in many circumstances. This means that you are called to welcome and interact with people in a manner that shows what it means to be a disciple of Christ. While all baptized people are called to practice lives of virtue, heeding this call is critical for lay ecclesial ministers. As a duly appointed minister of the church, you owe it to the church to be a person of upstanding character whose values are consistent with the gospel. You are accountable to your pastor, to the bishop, and to all those you serve. How you conduct yourself as you do your work is just as important as the end result of the work you are doing. Proclaiming the Good News of Jesus will have little effect unless the people receiving that message see you as a person of honesty, integrity, fidelity, and virtue. Be sure to contact your diocese to see if they have a code of ethical standards that lay ecclesial ministers are called to exemplify.

### Generosity, Dependability, Passion, and Compassion

We began this chapter by talking about the concept of a covenant relationship and the fact that your relationship with the Church is more than a business agreement or quid pro quo arrangement. As such, it calls you to approach your work with a generous and dependable heart, to go beyond the minimum and reach for the *magis*—the "more" that St. Ignatius talked about. You are also called to be someone who communicates a passion for the Gospel of Jesus Christ in a way that is authentic and consistent with your gifts and disposition. (Passion can be communicated in many ways and forms, ranging from a whisper to a shout!) Finally, the focus of your ministry should not be on your accomplishments but rather on the needs of God's people—which means that your approach must be driven by a sense of compassion.

You owe it to the church to minister dependably with generosity, passion, and compassion. God's grace has been poured out to you in such abundance that it is only right and just that you respond with a generous heart and spirit.

## What the Church Owes You

### A Written Role Description

As discussed earlier, your capabilities *do* have limits! The church owes you a written description of your specific responsibilities and your remuneration. If additional responsibilities are asked of you, it is fair to ask for additional compensation. A good role description or ministry profile that sets one up for success should include the following (drawn from *Employing Parish Catechetical Leaders: A Practical Handbook*, from the Wisconsin Directors of Religious Education Federation—WDREF):

- The title of your specific role (coordinator, director, etc.)
- Qualities and qualifications expected in your role (knowledge, abilities, skills)
- Identification as a salaried or nonsalaried position; full-time or part-time; and, if applicable, the minimum number of hours per week required to accomplish the assigned tasks
- The scope of your responsibility and the duties associated with it, which may include overseeing faith formation for some or all of the following groups as well as others:
    - Adults and young adults
    - Youth and teens
    - Elementary school students
    - Kindergarten and preschool students
    - Special-needs parishioners
    - Parochial school students
    - Vacation Bible School students
    - RCIA participants (children and adults)
    - Participants in family or intergenerational catechesis
    - Parishioners preparing for the Sacraments (baptism, reconciliation, first eucharist, confirmation, or marriage)
- A description of the evaluation process
- Details relating to salary and benefits (including health, dental, life/disability insurance, vacation, holidays, education allowance, retreat time and financial assistance, travel reimbursement, sick/personal days, bereavement days, retirement, ongoing formation,

unemployment compensation, family leave, portability of benefits, and so on)

- Identification of the superior to whom you report
- Term of position (10 or 12 months)
- Personnel you are responsible for supervising
- Administrative responsibilities
- Expectations for participation in parish, regional, diocesan, and national organizations

## A Fair and Living Wage and Adequate Benefits

While you did not enter this ministry as a way to get rich, you *are* owed a just wage that enables you to live comfortably and to provide for yourself and your family, and benefits that include adequate vacation time for maintaining your balance and letting your soul catch up with your body. The U.S. bishops assert that "All the moral principles that govern the just operation of any economic endeavor apply to the Church and its agencies and institutions; indeed, the Church should be exemplary" (*Economic Justice for All*, 347). They go on to say, "We bishops commit ourselves to the principle that those who serve the Church—laity, clergy, and religious—should receive a sufficient livelihood and the social benefits provided by responsible employers in our nation" (351). Canon law, too, requires that "administrators of temporal goods . . . are to pay those who work for them under contract 'a just and honest wage which would fittingly provide for their needs and those of their dependents'" (1286). This principle is further articulated in the church's Catholic social teaching, especially in regard to the principle of the Dignity of Work and the Rights of Workers. "If the dignity of work is to be protected," say the bishops, "then the basic rights of workers must be respected—the right to productive work, to decent and fair wages, to the organization and joining of unions, to private property, and to economic initiative" (*Sharing Catholic Social Teaching: Challenges and Directions*, USCCB).

In short, you have the right to ask for a wage and benefits that you consider fair.

## Time and Financial Support for Ongoing Formation

While you owe it to yourself to participate in ongoing formation, the church owes it to you to provide opportunities for such formation as well as the time and financial assistance to do so. Seminars, workshops, conferences, and course work all cost money and should not be a burden for you to shoulder. The parish and/or the diocese should provide financial assistance in the form of an annual allowance or scholarships for ongoing formation. In addition, your superiors should recognize that such formation takes time. Enough time should be granted for you to "sharpen the saw" without undue anxiety or pressure, both of which inhibit rather than foster spiritual and professional growth. Finally, paid time and funding for one or more retreat experiences per year should be included in your agreement. Retreat time is not a luxury; it is a necessary means by which a lay ecclesial minister's relationship with the Lord is given the prayerful time and attention it needs to flourish. Without this retreat time, we run the risk of forgetting that catechetical leadership is a vocation.

## Sound and Well-Articulated Policies

Although the church is not a business, it does conduct business, and your position is a part of that. Be sure you are informed of the relevant policies for hiring, termination, periodic evaluation, benefits, and safe environments, as well as canonical policies that apply to the catechetical ministry and various diocesan procedures, including due process for grievances (for example, when policies are not followed). Just a word on insisting on periodic formal evaluations: a pastor is not doing you a favor by waiving such an evaluation because he says you are doing so well. While such a waiver may feel very affirming, the unfortunate result is that your personnel file will remain empty. When the next pastor comes in, he will inherit no record of your performance, and you will be left with no grounds on which to build a case relating to your job performance, the scope of your position, or your salary, should questions arise. Periodic evaluations not only create an account of your service but also give you and your pastor or supervisor a chance to amend your role description, your responsibilities, and your remuneration as your role develops and changes in response to the ever-changing needs of the faith community. Following such an evaluation, a written summary from the pastor or supervisor should be shared with you and should become a part of your personnel file.

## Prayer, Support, and Affirmation

Once again, because your relationship with the church is not just a business arrangement but is also a covenant relationship, it is reasonable to expect that the church offer prayer, support, and affirmation for your ministry. It would be proper for the parish to publicly commission and install you as you begin your ministry, as well as to publicly recognize and affirm milestones along the way, including anniversaries of your installation and any certificates or degrees in ministry you might earn. In addition to a just wage and adequate benefits, which provide financial affirmation, the church owes you spiritual support and recognition for your generous service, too.

## Respect, Trust, Communication, and Collegiality

Because in its present form lay ecclesial ministry is still new to many, it is not uncommon for lay ecclesial ministers to feel that they are treated like second-class citizens compared to ordained clergy. The church owes it to you as a lay ecclesial minister to respect the unique circumstances and challenges you face as you seek to make a living in the secular world while serving the church. Yes, the role of the lay ecclesial minister is distinct from the role of the clergy, but it is a complementary role and worthy of respect and trust. Clergy and laity can and must work together in a spirit of mutuality and collegiality to use our gifts and our vocations to further the kingdom of God.

## The Church: Divine Yet Human

Interestingly enough, as I was working on this chapter, I asked many friends and colleagues what they believe lay ecclesial ministers owe the church and what the church owes its paid employees. The outstanding suggestions I received have shaped this chapter, and I am thankful to those who contributed ideas. Many were passionate in their responses, expressing strong opinions and very specific recommendations. Others, however, surprised me by insisting that the church "owes us nothing." (It is worth noting that these individuals were not lay ecclesial ministers but laypeople who are active in parish ministries.) Perhaps there are some readers of this book, too, who take umbrage at the notion of the church owing anything to its ministers.

My response is this: while it is true that we are owed nothing by God, the church is made up of human beings who are obligated, as Christians, to treat our fellow human beings fairly and justly. The church is the Body of Christ, but to keep the body healthy we are all—clergy and laity alike—called to enter into a relationship characterized by mutuality. In an ever-changing world, the church must continuously explore ever more meaningful and realistic ways to support those who minister in her name. Only in a true spirit of mutuality can we work together selflessly, thoughtfully, justly, and compassionately to proclaim the Good News of Jesus Christ to all of God's people.

## Summary: I Will Be Your God

*You shall be my people,*
*and I will be your God.* (Jer. 30:22)

Throughout Scripture, God continually invites his people into a covenant relationship with him. He asks us to be faithful to him, and he promises to love us and remain close to us no matter what. Our God is a God of mutuality and, as a catechetical leader and lay ecclesial minister, you have entered into a relationship of mutuality with the Catholic Church—a covenant relationship. For your part, you owe the Church competence, faithfulness, ongoing formational growth, virtue, and generosity. The Church, by the same token, owes you a specific role description, a just wage and benefits, ongoing formation, prayer, support, affirmation, and respect. Any relationship undertaken in a spirit of mutuality will survive and grow. The relationship of mutuality you have undertaken with the Church will enable you to grow and to contribute, in collaboration with the Church, to the furthering of God's kingdom.

## For Reflection and Discussion

- What relationships of mutuality do you enjoy in your own life? What have you contributed to those relationships, and what have you gained?
- What do you see yourself owing the church in your role as a lay ecclesial minister? What do you believe the church owes you?

## Growing as a Catechetical Leader

Pull out your role description or, if you don't have one, make a quick list of services you are being asked to "deliver" to your parish community and what it is that the Church will provide you in return. Is there a fair and equitable balance? Are there items that are not included that need to be?

Go to www.loyolapress.com/ECL to access the worksheet.

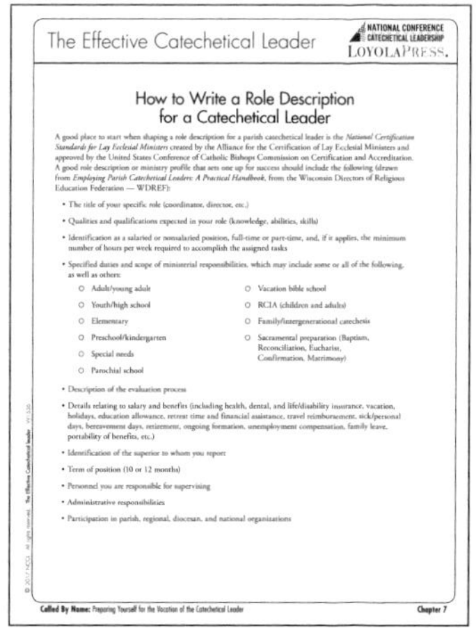

The Effective Catechetical Leader — NATIONAL CONFERENCE CATECHETICAL LEADERSHIP — LOYOLAPRESS.

How to Write a Role Description for a Catechetical Leader

A good place to start when shaping a role description for a parish catechetical leader is the *National Certification Standards for Lay Ecclesial Ministers* created by the Alliance for the Certification of Lay Ecclesial Ministers and approved by the United States Conference of Catholic Bishops Commission on Certification and Accreditation. A good role description or ministry profile that sets one up for success should include the following (drawn from *Employing Parish Catechetical Leaders: A Practical Handbook*, from the Wisconsin Directors of Religious Education Federation — WDREF):

- The title of your specific role (coordinator, director, etc.)
- Qualities and qualifications expected in your role (knowledge, abilities, skills)
- Identification as a salaried or nonsalaried position, full-time or part-time, and, if it applies, the minimum number of hours per week required to accomplish the assigned tasks
- Specified duties and scope of ministerial responsibilities, which may include some or all of the following, as well as others:
  - Adult/young adult
  - Youth/high school
  - Elementary
  - Preschool/kindergarten
  - Special needs
  - Parochial school
  - Vacation bible school
  - RCIA (children and adults)
  - Family/intergenerational catechesis
  - Sacramental preparation (Baptism, Reconciliation, Eucharist, Confirmation, Matrimony)
- Description of the evaluation process
- Details relating to salary and benefits (including health, dental, and life/disability insurance, vacation, holidays, education allowance, retreat time and financial assistance, travel reimbursement, sick/personal days, bereavement days, retirement, ongoing formation, unemployment compensation, family leave, portability of benefits, etc.)
- Identification of the superior to whom you report
- Term of position (10 or 12 months)
- Personnel you are responsible for supervising
- Administrative responsibilities
- Participation in parish, regional, diocesan, and national organizations



**Called By Name:** Preparing Yourself for the Vocation of the Catechetical Leader — **Chapter 7**

## Suggested Action

Perhaps up until now, you've not given much thought to what it is that the Church owes you in this relationship of mutuality. Take some time to compose a letter to the Church (that you will not deliver) in which you express in personal terms (not legal terms) what it is that you need from the Church in order to be effective in your role as a catechetical leader. Consider sharing this with a peer or a spiritual companion or director and use it to shape your thinking for your next performance review. Remember: in a relationship of mutuality, a performance review should be about the performance of *both* parties.

## For Further Consideration

To further explore the topic of this chapter, consider the following resources:

*The Changing Face of the Church: Emerging Models of Parish Leadership*. Marti R. Jewell and David A. Ramey (Chicago: Loyola Press, 2010).

*National Certification Standards for Lay Ecclesial Ministry.* (The Alliance for the Certification of Lay Ecclesial Ministers/ USCCB, Washington, D.C., 2011).

*Employing Parish Catechetical Leaders: A Practical Handbook.* (Wisconsin Directors of Religious Education Federation, Grantsburg, WI, 2008).

# 8

# From Surviving to Thriving: Maintaining Personal and Professional Balance

One of the first instances of what is now called "ministry burnout" is recorded in the book of 1 Kings, chapters 18 and 19. There, we find good old Elijah, whose successes seem overshadowed by failures, wandering in the desert in a state of total despair and exhaustion. Finally he collapses under a broom tree and says to God, "It is enough; now O LORD, take away my life, for I am no better than my ancestors" (1 Kings 19:4). Elijah is burned out. The story, thankfully, has a happy ending: God hears his cry for help and sends an angel to twice awaken him and give him something to eat and drink. Fortified by the nourishment that God provides, Elijah finds the strength to continue on his journey.

## I Have Had Enough, Lord!

You will have moments like this as a catechetical minister! No one is exempt from the realities of burnout, since we are all humans with limitations. The best we can do is to be aware of the factors that contribute to burnout, engage in practices that minimize the potential of harm from burnout, and take healing measures when burnout comes to pass.

You are most likely familiar with the yin-yang symbol, which represents, among other things, the dynamic balance of opposite yet complementary energies. It is a visual expression of the idea that there are two sides to every coin. Although the two sides are unique and different from one another, they are also interdependent and can never be separated. Night and day are good examples: each is different from the other, but together they create a whole, and neither would make much sense without the other. In Chinese philosophy, there is not only balance between the yin and the yang but also harmony, which is achieved when the two energies or realities blend into a seamless totality. The goal in life is always to seek balance and harmony.

In the Christian tradition, harmony is referred to as *peace*—that state of being in which different and even opposing realities and energies come into harmony with one another. We find peace when our will and the will of God are aligned in our heart. We find peace when heaven and earth meet, as they do in the Incarnation—which is why the angels sing "Glory to God in the highest heaven, and on earth peace" at the birth of Jesus (Luke 2:14).

The goal of the spiritual life is to actively seek this peace. As a catechetical leader, you are called to seek this peace in your own heart and to lead others to seek this peace in their lives—and in society at large—by aligning our wills with the will of God. "Thy kingdom come, thy will be done," Jesus taught us to pray, "on earth as it is in heaven."

An important part of your role as a catechetical leader, then, is finding and maintaining personal and professional balance. Just as physical therapists help people strengthen specific muscles so they can keep their balance, remain stable, and avoid falls, catechetical leaders must strengthen specific spiritual muscles to remain stable in their vocation and avoid the common pitfalls of ministry. To this end, we'll first look at some aspects of pastoral ministry that can sap your energy and lead to burnout. Then we'll identify some strategies for minimizing the possibility of burnout and—should it happen—recovering from its harmful effects.

## There's No End in Sight!

In catechetical ministry, it often feels as if there is no end in sight, simply because there *is* no end! Your ministry will never be finished, and there's even a good chance you'll find yourself working on the Sabbath, the "day of rest." The endless nature of the work can be a steady drain on your energy unless you take time to restore it. To combat this danger, be sure to schedule pauses and breaks from your ministry so that you can replenish your energy for your ongoing journey, just as Elijah did.

## Am I Making a Difference?

The outcomes of ministry are rarely immediate and often intangible. In other professions, one can usually tell when a project has begun and when it is finished: when the product or service has been delivered. In your work as a catechetical leader, though, a lot of loose ends never really get tied up. You find yourself doing all kinds of things for people, both on and off the record, and then wondering if any of it is making a difference. Often you will never know, and over time this ambiguity can dampen your enthusiasm. Therefore, it is a good idea to engage in projects or hobbies that involve clearly defined tasks and offer concrete results. When I began in ministry, for example, I needed to supplement my income, so I worked part-time at my uncle's drugstore. I enjoyed setting up displays, stocking shelves, waiting on customers, and working on other projects that provided immediate gratification and a sense of accomplishment. Today I stay engaged in hobbies and home-improvement projects for the same reason. Who knew cleaning out the garage could be so valuable to my spiritual well-being?

## This Feels like a Merry-Go-Round

No sooner does one catechetical year end than you find yourself preparing to launch the next! Ministry—especially the catechetical ministry—is cyclical and repetitive. You do the same things over and over, year after year. There are plusses and minuses to this. On the one hand, repetition offers chances to improve from year to year. On the other hand, the routine can grow wearisome. Try to find ways to change things up every year without necessarily rocking the boat. Keep things fresh by adding some new twists and turns to your program such as a new resource or component to be used in every lesson. In your personal life, do things to break up the routine—especially things that have nothing at all to do with your ministry, such as departures from your routine or various forms of entertainment or physical exercise.

## Heal Yourselves!

There is a powerful scene in the musical *Jesus Christ Superstar* in which the character of Jesus, overwhelmed by the people crowding around him and asking him for healing, screams, "Heal yourselves!" While Jesus, of course, never said this, it is indeed a typical human response for those of us working in service professions. People will come to you constantly with expectations and needs. And the fact is, as a minister you most likely see yourself as a helper. And yet you do have limits. It will be important for you to build in time for solitude so that you are not always surrounded (or hounded!) by people with expectations. In solitude you can spend time with yourself and the Lord, allowing him to replenish your spirit.

## Tired of the Same Ol' Faces

In ministry, as in other professions, you can find yourself seeing the same faces day in and day out. Even if you like them, you can't get away from them. And, of course, if you *don't* get along with the faces you see every day, the going can get tough. As a catechetical leader, it is crucial that you nurture healthy relationships outside your ministry. Make it a regular commitment to spend time with people who neither know nor care what the words *catechetical, pedagogical*, or *ecclesial* mean!

## Who's Gonna Take Care of Me?

People in service professions spend great amounts of time and energy catering to the needs of others. In fact, caring for others defines who we are. It can therefore be difficult to recognize when we ourselves need care and attention, as we all do from time to time. One major temptation pastoral ministers can fall prey to is seeking attention from those we minister to. This is not only unhealthy, it is also dangerous. For example, it can lead to seeking intimacy from someone who is underage. To avoid these risks, be sure to maintain relationships outside your ministerial world that provide you with comfort and support. Consider a spiritual director—someone who can offer you undivided attention and help you focus on your own journey as you devote attention to those you serve.

## Can I Say What I Really Feel?

I mentioned earlier that I spent time working in my uncle's drugstore. There, I was taught to be kind, polite, and attentive to the customers, since they were the ones who ultimately paid my salary. Of course, this was not always easy, especially when a customer was being difficult or I had worked a long, busy shift. I used to joke with my uncle and say, "Wouldn't it be nice if just once a year we could tell customers what we were really feeling?" In ministry, the same can be true. In many ways, the pastoral minister is called to put on a persona. While that may sound as if you're being phony, you're not. For example, if you happen to be an introvert and you must spend an entire evening interacting with parents at a gathering, it can be extremely trying. Your inner voice may be screaming, *Can't we just go home?!* while your leadership position requires you to be friendly, welcoming, and outgoing. It's important for you to know your own limits—and to know your own personality type. For years I did not realize that I am technically an introvert. This doesn't make me shy; it just means that my energy is depleted by social interaction and is restored in solitude. Once you are in touch with the basic truths of your personality, you can strive to maintain a balance that works for you.

## I'm a Loser

The Beatles had a popular song in the 1960s titled "I'm a Loser." No doubt that's what Elijah was thinking when he collapsed under that broom tree and asked the Lord to take his life. From time to time in pastoral ministry, we can feel like out-and-out failures. I remember planning an Advent gathering for the young adults who played volleyball in our parish gym each week. I talked it up for weeks. Folks nodded and smiled and said they would come. The night of the event, I sat alone in the chapel as dozens of young adults played volleyball in the gym next door, totally uninterested in what I was offering. Of course, I felt like a complete failure. It's important to separate ourselves from both our achievements and our failures and to learn from each of them. Likewise, it is important to celebrate our successes—whether big or small—so that we can offset the feelings of failure that will inevitably occur.

## Maintaining Your Spiritual Balance in Catechetical Ministry

The truth is that catechetical leaders must work hard to maintain balance and spiritual wellness. In my book *7 Keys to Spiritual Wellness*,

I identify seven ways any Christian can do this; each way provides immunity against one of the "Seven Deadly Sins." It is important to know that in public ministry, the temptation to commit the seven deadly sins is heightened—which means that our responsibility to remain vigilant against them is also heightened. Let's take a look at these seven keys for spiritual wellness, which I've adapted here for your ministry as a catechetical leader.

1. **See yourself as you really are.** As a lay ecclesial minister, you are called to do God's work, and you are made in the image of God. However, you are not God! Thinking otherwise was the downfall of Adam and Eve. One common temptation for lay ecclesial ministers is to develop a "messiah complex"—imagining that everything depends on us instead of recognizing that all things depend on God. When we take ourselves too seriously and develop an overinflated sense of self-importance, our relationships with others suffer. We develop an inability to listen to authority, to take criticism, to admit being wrong, or to ask for help. We experience an increase in anxiety, self-pity, anger, jealousy, and insecurity. We find ourselves becoming overly legalistic, critical of others, defensive, and negative, and we suffer a loss of compassion.

   So, as a catechetical leader, it is imperative that you cultivate a sense of humility, following the example of Jesus, who washed the feet of his disciples, and of Mary, his mother, who responded to God's call by saying, "My soul magnifies the Lord." As theologian Bishop Robert Barron writes, "Either your life is about Jesus and his mission or it is about you. There is no third option" (*The Strangest Way*, Orbis, 125). And it is that first option—a life that is about Jesus and his mission—that is the only surefire way to serve effectively as a catechetical leader.

2. **Actively seek the good of others.** It's human nature for us to compare ourselves to others. It begins when we are children wondering why someone has a bigger, shinier toy than ours, and it continues as we grow older and wonder why someone has nicer clothes, a bigger house, a more expensive car, fewer wrinkles, or a slimmer waist than we have. So I guess I shouldn't have been surprised when, as a catechetical leader, I noticed that many pastoral ministers had the bad habit of comparing themselves with one another. When a fellow catechetical leader asked about my schedule and I mentioned that I took Tuesdays off, she snidely replied, "That must be nice"—as though she could never afford such a luxury because of her myriad responsibilities.

   One great way to lose your balance as a catechetical leader is to compare yourself with your peers and to see them as rivals and competitors, which results in bitterness about their good fortune (think Cain and Abel) and delight at their failures. It also causes us to read false motives into others' words and actions and become prone to gossip, which can be rampant in ministerial circles. Instead of heading down this slippery slope, we are called to see our fellow ministers as partners. The key to developing this ability is to recognize, as did St. Paul, that God's grace is sufficient for you (2 Cor. 12:9). Likewise, St. Ignatius of Loyola was able to pray, "Give me only your love and your grace, that is enough for me." When you can do this, you will be able to actively seek the good of others and avoid being threatened by them.
3. **Think before acting.** In your role as a catechetical leader, you will find yourself challenged by conflicts of various sorts: conflicts with coworkers, the pastor, a catechist, a parent, and so on. Some of these situations will push you to the limit. Perhaps the most important thing you can do as a catechetical leader is to

learn how to breathe! When we simply react in the heat of a conflict without taking a moment to breathe and gather our thoughts, three unfortunate things tend to happen: the response comes out too quickly, it is excessive, and the effects last too long. Strong emotions such as anger do not possess good judgment. Left to its own devices, anger is reactive and unreflective, and its ultimate goal is the destruction of the object or person who has aroused it.

This is why anger-management strategies almost always include taking a few deep breaths and counting to ten before responding. A ten-second time-out can provide the brain with just the time it needs to intervene and save you from yourself.

4. **Hold on loosely.** Stress and anxiety are a part of life, and the catechetical ministry is not immune to these realities. Because pastoral ministry does not always culminate in tangible results, we can grow anxious about whether the seeds we are sowing today will take root and blossom in the future. One temptation we have when experiencing this brand of anxiety is to fill the void of uncertainty by acquiring things. When we amass possessions, we gain a false sense of control over the tangible world, and our hunger for tangibles is temporarily satisfied. But the satisfaction is short-lived—and then we need more.

   So when a certain emptiness gnaws within, we may find ourselves repeatedly drawn to activities like shopping, eating, drinking, gambling, playing video games, surfing the Internet, or watching reality TV. In and of themselves, most of these activities are not bad. However, when done to excess, they can become minor addictions—easy fixes when we crave tangible satisfaction. Detachment, on the other hand, is the recognition that nothing but the grace of God can truly fill the empty space within us. One way to foster a spirit of detachment in our lives is by practicing "Ignatian indifference." St. Ignatius taught that when we recognize that our reason for living is to be in intimate communion with God, we can become "indifferent" to everything else. This doesn't mean we become apathetic or uncaring. Instead, it means we avoid growing overly invested in created, tangible things. St. Ignatius says that this attitude of indifference—detachment—permits us to accept whatever comes.

Jesus knew that we acquire possessions—our adult security blankets—to compensate for the insecurities and fears that come with our imagined independence. So to help us trust God, Jesus offered us a prayer that we can think of as our "Declaration of *De*pendence"—the Lord's Prayer. In this prayer, we admit our total dependence on God for direction in our lives, for our daily bread, for forgiveness, for relief from temptation, and for deliverance from evil. We pray to let go of our own will and embrace that of the Lord.

In the end, the spiritual life is all about letting go instead of holding on. That's why Jesus said that the greatest love—the most generous act of all—is to lay down one's life for another. To lay down one's life simply means to let go of yourself and your own ego, to trust in the wisdom of God, and to put the good of others before your own. This can be done only when we hold on loosely to the things of this world. As a catechetical leader, your hands must always be empty so that you can reach out and hold on to God and to invite others to do the same.

5. **Recognize and set limits.** Please accept this fact right now: while your love of Jesus may have no bounds, your physical and emotional self *does*! One of the greatest temptations for pastoral ministers is to fail to recognize and set limits and boundaries. You will be tempted to say yes to every request that comes your way because, by nature, you want to serve. The truth is, one of the healthiest things you can do for yourself and for others as a

lay ecclesial minister is to learn that you do not need to say yes to every request that comes your way. Sometimes, you need to say no.

- First, you need to set boundaries and limits on your time so that you avoid burnout. Be sure to schedule downtime, regular days off, and regular vacations so that your breaks are predictable and not haphazard. Practice saying "no" to smaller requests that can be handled by someone else—and do not feel compelled to give extensive explanations for your response.
- It is likewise critical for you to set limits on how you "let off steam" or "take off the edge" in response to the stress of your ministry. It is a sad reality that some pastoral ministers find solace in eating and drinking to excess to dull the senses when the going gets rough. There are two ways of gauging when any type of behavior has crossed over into the realm of excess:
    - *The behavior has become counterproductive to the individual doing it.* For example, you might want to cheer yourself up by going shopping and buying something for yourself. This indeed can be a pick-me-up. Taken to excess, however, the bills that accompany a shopping binge can cause feelings of guilt and depression. So much for cheering yourself up.
    - *The behavior has become persistent.* Despite the eventual letdown, the behavior gives us a boost, so we continue to practice it. More of the behavior or substance may be required each time to get similar results.

If these describe a coping strategy you've developed, it's time to seek a new strategy.

- Finally, it is absolutely crucial that you recognize and respect limits and boundaries in relationships. It is all too common for pastoral ministers to seek intimacy, understanding, and attention from those they minister to. When this happens between adults, it is unhealthy and, if it involves someone in a married relationship, can be immoral. When this involves someone who is underage, it can lead to a criminal act. Setting and respecting boundaries are integral to being a healthy and effective pastoral minister. Be sure to check with your diocese for guidelines on setting boundaries and ensuring a safe environment.

6. **Seek beauty.** It's a pretty good bet (and highly encouraged!) that you are thinking about taking a vacation somewhere along the line, perhaps during a break or at the end of the catechetical year. And no doubt you are dreaming about vacationing somewhere beautiful, such as the Grand Canyon, the Great Smoky Mountains, the Bahamas, Puerto Rico, or Marco Island. In fact, our souls crave beauty. The problem is that we tend to limit our experience of beauty to a couple of weeks per year—or imagine it is unavailable to us altogether. But beauty is all around us if only we open our eyes.

   Gandhi once said, "When I admire the wonder of a sunset or the beauty of the moon, my soul expands in worship of the creator." In other words, beauty can not only expand our soul but also transport us beyond ourselves. Unlike other animals in God's creation, we human beings desire to transcend ourselves—to be transported beyond the merely physical and material into the realm of the spiritual. We seek to encounter mystery—to touch mystery and to be touched by it. And that which is beautiful somehow also possesses mystery. So, we are attracted to beauty in hopes that we will be able to touch mystery and, in doing so, be loved and embraced by it.

As a catechetical leader, you need to make sure your soul experiences moments of expansion, transcendence, and mystery—because many aspects of our work can have the opposite effect. Take advantage of the many ways God's beauty is available to you: in nature (gardening, fishing, hiking, camping), in music (all varieties), in the visual arts, in athleticism (both developing your own and admiring others'), in literature, and so on. To maintain your balance as a catechetical leader, I encourage you to reflect on all the ways you consciously seek and encounter beauty in your life and to commit yourself to recognizing this beauty as a reflection of God's beauty, which is the object of our deepest and most passionate desires.

7. **Unleash your imagination.** This is perhaps the most important thing you can do to maintain your balance as an effective catechetical leader. It takes great imagination to proclaim the Good News of the kingdom of God to a world that can't recognize it at best and doesn't believe in it at worst. Your job as a catechetical leader is to set people's hearts on fire. In chapter 2, we introduced the "good kind of heartburn"—the kind the two disciples on the road to Emmaus experienced as Jesus walked with them (Luke 24:32). The question is, what gives you heartburn? What sparks a fire in your heart? What two sticks are you rubbing together in hopes of igniting such a fire? Answer that—and do more of it—and you'll be on the right track to maintaining your balance.

As a catechetical leader, you are called to share Christ's vision of a hoped-for reality—an alternate reality—that Jesus referred to as the kingdom of God. It is a vision of a world that exists somewhere beyond what our eyes can presently see. It is a longing for *magis*, for "something more." In order to envision this alternate, "something more" reality, one needs an active imagination: not a flight of fancy but the ability to see reality as it is while also seeing another reality that lies beyond the indifference, cynicism, and relativism that cloud our collective twenty-first-century vision. A good way to jump-start your imagination is by exercising that part of the brain where imagination is located—the right brain—by regularly engaging in activities such as reading, drawing or painting, looking at and responding to art, working with your hands, listening to music or playing a musical instrument, enjoying theater, cooking, meditating, and interacting with children, who are the true masters of imagination!

## Summary: I Am Weary

*If I say, "I will not mention him,*
*or speak any more in his name,"*
*then within me there is something like a burning fire*
*shut up in my bones;*
*I am weary with holding it in,*
*and I cannot.* (Jer. 20:9)

The prophet Jeremiah experienced burnout. Considering all the hardships he endured—including being thrown into a cistern (Jer. 38)—this makes pretty good sense. And yet his fire for God had not totally gone out. In fact, he admits that the fire burns in such a way that he cannot hold it; he must hand it to others. In your ministry as a catechetical leader, I hope you will not be thrown into a cistern. But many aspects of the ministry will drain you. You will grow weary, and you may experience burnout. For these reasons, it is extremely important that you maintain your own personal and professional balance. Take precautions to avoid pitfalls and temptations, and take steps to recover from moments of weakness and weariness when they occur.

## For Reflection and Discussion

- Which of the aspects of ministry described in the first half of the chapter tend to get the best of you? How do you respond?
- What can you do to prevent these aspects of ministry from getting the best of you? What can you do to rebound when they do?

## Growing as a Catechetical Leader

Which of the seven keys for spiritual wellness are you already proficient in? Which need more work?

Go to www.loyolapress.com/ECL to access the worksheet.

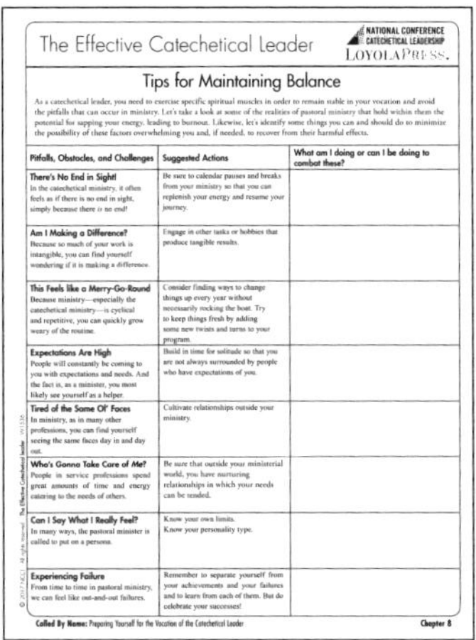

The Effective Catechetical Leader

NATIONAL CONFERENCE CATECHETICAL LEADERSHIP

LOYOLAPRESS.

Tips for Maintaining Balance

As a catechetical leader, you need to exercise specific spiritual muscles in order to remain stable in your vocation and avoid the pitfalls that can occur in ministry. Let's take a look at some of the realities of pastoral ministry that hold within them the potential for sapping your energy, leading to burnout. Likewise, let's identify some things you can and should do to minimize the possibility of these factors overwhelming you and, if needed, to recover from their harmful effects.

| Pitfalls, Obstacles, and Challenges | Suggested Actions | What am I doing or can I be doing to combat these? |
|---|---|---|
| **There's No End in Sight!** In the catechetical ministry, it often feels as if there is no end in sight, simply because there *is* no end! | Be sure to calendar pauses and breaks from your ministry so that you can replenish your energy and resume your journey. | |
| **Am I Making a Difference?** Because so much of your work is intangible, you can find yourself wondering if it is making a difference. | Engage in other tasks or hobbies that produce tangible results. | |
| **This Feels like a Merry-Go-Round** Because ministry—especially the catechetical ministry—is cyclical and repetitive, you can quickly grow weary of the routine. | Consider finding ways to change things up every year without necessarily rocking the boat. Try to keep things fresh by adding some new twists and turns to your program. | |
| **Expectations Are High** People will constantly be coming to you with expectations and needs. And the fact is, as a minister, you most likely see yourself as a helper. | Build in time for solitude so that you are not always surrounded by people who have expectations of you. | |
| **Tired of the Same Ol' Faces** In ministry, as in many other professions, you can find yourself seeing the same faces day in and day out. | Cultivate relationships outside your ministry. | |
| **Who's Gonna Take Care of Me?** People in service professions spend great amounts of time and energy catering to the needs of others. | Be sure that outside your ministerial world, you have nurturing relationships in which your needs can be tended. | |
| **Can I Say What I Really Feel?** In many ways, the pastoral minister is called to put on a persona. | Know your own limits. Know your personality type. | |
| **Experiencing Failure** From time to time in pastoral ministry, we can feel like out-and-out failures. | Remember to separate yourself from your achievements and your failures and to learn from each of them. But do celebrate your successes! | |



**Called By Name:** Preparing Yourself for the Vocation of the Catechetical Leader **Chapter 8**

## Suggested Action

Over the next seven weeks, commit to focusing each week on one of the seven keys to spiritual wellness. Pray about this particular key, and ask God for the grace you need to maintain your spiritual balance.

## For Further Consideration

To further explore the topic of this chapter, consider the following resources:

*Ministry Burnout.* John A. Sanford (Mahwah, NJ: Paulist Press, 1992).

*Zeal without Burnout.* Christopher Ash (Surrey, UK: The Good Book Company, 2016).

*Resilient Ministry: What Pastors Told Us About Surviving and Thriving.* Bob Burns, Tasha D. Chapman, and Donald Guthrie (Downers Grove, IL: InterVarsity Press, 2013).

*Evangelii Gaudium.* Pope Francis (2013).

*Boundary Setting for Clergy and Ministry Workers.* Jim Stout (San Antonio, TX: Shepherd Publishing, 2016).

# 9

# Not "Me and God" but "We and God": Finding Support

For years, I've been saying that for Catholics, "faith is less of a 'me and God' experience and more of a 'we and God' experience." Interestingly enough, several years ago, I found myself at a lecture being given by a Protestant minister to a primarily Protestant audience. At one point, he shared the following observation: "You know, we Protestants tend to take more of a 'me and God' approach to our faith while our Catholic brothers and sisters take more of a 'we and God' approach." I was so tickled to hear him affirm what I had suspected for so long that I nearly broke into applause—but then decided that might blow my cover as the lone Catholic in the crowd!

## A Profound Sense of Community

The truth of the matter, however, is that our Catholic understanding of community is profound—so profound that we believe that even death does not separate us (i.e., we believe in the communion of saints). At Mass, we stand together, kneel together, sit together, bow together, bless ourselves together, and respond together. We drink from the same cup at communion time. Even in private, when we pray the Liturgy of the Hours, we are not praying alone since we are joined with many others praying the same words at the same time in the privacy of their own homes. Everywhere we go, we "have the network" with us (as a mobile phone service once advertised).

All of this is to say that there are a variety of networks (in addition to the communion of saints) from which you can draw help and support as a Catholic catechetical leader. In this chapter, we'll explore some of the various groups that you can and should benefit from in your catechetical ministry.

## Real Relationships

When I was a high school religion teacher, we used to joke about how much we liked being teachers on days when the students weren't present, such as teacher in-service days. Of course, while it was nice to have a break, the reality is that teachers love teaching precisely because of the students and the time spent with them, as challenging and exhausting as that time can be. In his book *The Holy Longing*, Ronald Rolheiser, OMI, says that spirituality is ultimately communitarian and that it is only through the "grounding, earthiness, and necessary pain" of relationships that we find true balance. While you belong to a parish family as a catechetical leader, it is important that you establish relationships that exist beyond that community—relationships that help you to "keep it real."

Supportive relationships are healthy for us, not just emotionally and spiritually but also physically. Several studies—in particular, the *Grant Study* from Harvard Medical School and the *Terman Study of the Gifted* from Stanford University—indicate that the presence of supportive relationships is a key factor in living a long, happy life. In fact, health scientist Howard Friedman, author of *The Longevity Project*, insists that the single most important recommendation he can make for living a longer, healthier, happier life is not to begin a rigorous exercise program but to connect with and help others. I can tell you from personal experience that forming and keeping supportive relationships was one of several keys to my success as a parish catechetical leader and continues to be important today. Let's take a look at some of these relationships.

## The Local Cluster, Deanery, or Vicariate Group of Catechetical Leaders

If it weren't for the River Oaks Cluster of DREs, I don't know where I would be today. When I was forced to leave teaching because the archdiocese was closing my school, I found myself in parish ministry as a pastoral associate and DRE in the southeast suburbs of Chicago, trying to find my way as a catechetical leader. In no time, I received an invitation to join a cluster of DREs for breakfast or lunch at Denny's once a month. There, I met Pat, Sharon, Betty, and other seasoned catechetical leaders who took me under their wings and showed me the ropes as I stumbled and bumbled through my first years in parish ministry. Decades later, I am still friends with many of these wonderful people. It was enjoyable to spend time with peers, sharing our experiences, venting our frustrations, voicing our joys, and asking how on earth we were supposed to do what God had called us to do.

It wasn't all just socializing however. We put our heads together to "get stuff done" as well. We collaborated on regional catechist formation, gathering catechists from our eight or so parishes and pooling our resources to bring in talented speakers to energize and equip the troops. And later, when many of us found ourselves taking on the RCIA process in our parishes too, we collaborated to plan and host regional Welcome Rites, which were held at a different parish each year.

Often, local gatherings of catechetical leaders are informal and materialize out of sheer necessity as pastoral ministers reach out and turn to their nearest neighbors for help. Such clusters not only provide members with friendship and support but also create models of collaboration between parishes that can be useful to other ministries with similarly limited resources. Once relationships are established and missions emerge, members of a cluster often schedule annual retreats together. Taking a collective pause can enrich the renewal experience and provide the needed inspiration to face the ongoing challenges of catechetical ministry.

If you are new to the catechetical ministry, contact your neighboring catechetical leaders and find out whether a local cluster exists. Participating in one (or starting one!) can give you the kind of support you need not only to survive but also to thrive in your vocation.

## The Local or Regional Professional Organization of Catechetical Leaders

- In Chicago, it's called CARE—the Chicago Association of Religious Educators.
- In Wisconsin, it's called WDREF—the Wisconsin Directors of Religious Education Federation.
- In Des Moines, Iowa, it's called CLADD—the Catechetical Leadership Association for the Diocese of Des Moines.
- In Eastern Pennsylvania, it's called the EPDRE—the Eastern Pennsylvania Directors of Religious Education.

At the local or regional level, you can find more formal professional organizations of catechetical leaders. These groups provide members with the resources and opportunities to further develop their own professionalism. Such organizations, which often require a membership fee, advocate for professionalism in the catechetical ministry, study key issues related to the catechetical ministry and recommend new approaches and strategies, research and make recommendations about church policies and catechetical issues, facilitate communication among members and with other ministries and organizations, and provide ongoing formation for members.

On a personal note, some of my favorite and most fulfilling experiences as a speaker and presenter have happened at professional conferences where catechetical leaders have gathered to assess the present state of our beloved ministry and to share visions for its future. I strongly encourage you to take the time to find an association in your diocese, region, or state—either by talking to colleagues or contacting your local catechetical office—and then get involved in it! You'll be glad you did.

## The National Conference for Catechetical Leadership (NCCL)

Every spring since the early 1990s, I have eagerly awaited the annual NCCL conference, held in various cities across the country (visit www.nccl.org), which gives me a chance to spend time and rub elbows with some of the most gifted catechetical ministers in the country.

The NCCL is the only independent national organization in the United States dedicated exclusively to serving the church's catechetical mission. It does so by assisting catechetical leaders in "achieving competence as leaders in the ministries of evangelization and catechesis within the teaching mission of the multi-cultural Catholic Church in the United States." The organization

- promotes the ministries of catechesis and evangelization;
- collaborates with the bishops and other ministerial organizations;
- nurtures the spiritual, professional, and personal development of catechetical leaders; and
- gathers catechetical ministers at levels ranging from diocesan and provincial to regional and national.

Today, more than 90 percent of all dioceses and eparchies (Eastern Catholic equivalent of a diocese) are represented in the membership of NCCL, along with other diocesan and provincial associations of parish catechetical leaders and Catholic publishing houses. Membership is composed of bishops, pastors, diocesan catechetical directors (and their staffs), parish directors of religious education, academics, and publishers of catechetical materials. Members from different walks of life participate for various reasons, but they all receive the same benefits: a connection with professional peers across the country; exposure to cutting-edge ideas, resources, and catechetical approaches; and opportunities for their own professional development.

I look forward to attending the NCCL conference each spring to meet up with my "same time, next year" friends and colleagues. It is very much like an annual homecoming. Each year, a group of us catechetical professionals from Chicago get together to enjoy a meal and catch up. (We joke about how we have to travel to a distant city each year in order to get together!) The opportunity to network and hobnob with "fellow wizards" in the catechetical ministry *and* be exposed to some of the most talented catechetical speakers in the world is priceless. For me, the experience of attending the annual NCCL conference is much like a sacred pilgrimage—a spiritual journey to a sacred site (made sacred by the noble mission of the catechetical ministry) in order to deepen one's faith and grow closer to God. I highly recommend becoming a member of NCCL and attending the annual conference—"same time, next year"!

## Regional Conferences

In addition to the annual NCCL conference, catechetical leaders can find support at a number of regional catechetical conferences. These conferences also draw very fine speakers and offer valuable networking opportunities. Even if your own diocese or region regularly hosts such a conference, you should keep several additional ones on your radar:

- Los Angeles Religious Education Congress (Anaheim, CA)
- Mid-Atlantic Congress (Baltimore, MD)
- Gulf Coast Faith Formation Conference (New Orleans, LA)
- St. John Bosco Conference (Steubenville, OH)
- University of Dallas Ministry Conference (Dallas, TX)

These and other major conferences—as well as smaller conferences hosted by dioceses all over the country—provide catechetical leaders with opportunities to network with peers, grow in faith, and explore strategies for more effective catechetical ministry. Check one out in the coming year—and take a friend!

## Spiritual Direction

I discussed spiritual direction in an earlier chapter, and because I find it so valuable, I'd like to return to it now. I find spiritual direction to be one of the most valuable ways of keeping my spirituality on the "front burner" of my consciousness, and I believe strongly that anyone involved in lay ecclesial ministry should reap the benefits of regular spiritual direction. You can trust me on this, because I have been visiting the same spiritual director on a monthly basis since 2003! I have also completed a certificate program in spiritual direction and now provide direction for several directees on a regular basis.

"How exactly does spiritual direction work?" you may be wondering. A typical session—usually once a month—lasts approximately one hour. During that time, the director and the directee enter into a prayerful atmosphere where they can be attentive to the Holy Spirit, who is the real "director." For the most part, the director listens as the directee shares, looking back over recent events to explore how God has been present or probing issues that are on the mind and in the heart. Occasionally, prompted by the Spirit, the director will question, challenge, or support the directee. The director may also suggest reading materials, reflection questions, or spiritual exercises in anticipation of future sessions.

Spiritual direction is a trusting relationship in which a trained and competent guide "companions" another person or persons. (Spiritual direction is usually one-on-one, but group spiritual direction is also available.) A spiritual director listens closely and then gives feedback about what he or she is hearing and sensing about the movement of the Holy Spirit in a person's life. Such feedback is for an individual's consideration only; the spiritual director is not a guru who tells you what you must do. Instead, a spiritual director is someone who walks with you as you discover God's presence, action, and direction for your life.

Spiritual direction can play a vital role in the life of a catechetical leader. It can help you maintain your own spiritual health by getting in touch with your soul and allowing it to feed you. If you feel "funny" about sharing private experiences with a professional spiritual guide, remember that spiritual direction has been a part of the Christian tradition since its beginnings. Although it may be outside your current comfort zone, you can trust that many of the wisest and most effective Catholic teachers over the course of centuries have sought similar relationships—not with the expectation of finding a "warm fuzzy" friend but of finding God.

In short, spiritual direction can provide the following:

- A companion who will supportively and attentively listen to you as you talk about your relationship with God;
- A trained professional who will help you spot resistances and obstacles—and desires and attractions—in your spiritual life;
- An opportunity to know yourself better, become more attuned to God's presence, and respond more fully to that presence in your life;

- A deeper awareness of the presence and action of God in your everyday life;
- An opportunity to evaluate your priorities and discern how God is inviting, urging, and confirming you;
- An opportunity to explore new ways to pray or to rediscover your prayer life;
- An opportunity to develop a sense of connectedness and to honor and savor your experiences of God.

In much the same way that Jesus gave “heartburn” to the two disciples on the road to Emmaus (Luke 24:32), a spiritual director can help you stoke the fire that is your passion for living as a disciple of Christ and calling others to do so in your role as a catechetical leader.

## Key Relationships

While building relationships is a crucial part of your ministry as a catechetical leader, maintaining supportive relationships in your personal life is critical for your spiritual and emotional well-being—and for the well-being of your ministry. Be sure to pay attention to and seek support from the following key relationships in your life, in addition to the ones we’ve already explored in this chapter:

- Your relationship with your spouse or significant other;
- Your relationship with your children;
- Your relationship with your siblings and other close relatives;
- Your relationship with good friends;
- Your relationship with someone you consider a mentor;
- Your relationship with your peers; and
- Your relationship with your faith community.

Ultimately, leadership is about people in relationship. If you want to be an effective catechetical leader, then you must pay attention to your own relationships. In the Nicene Creed, we say that we believe Jesus is "one in being with the Father" and that the Holy Spirit "proceeds from the Father and the Son." This means that we understand God not as an individual but as a community of love. In other words, God's very essence is loving relationship. When we say that God is love—which is something we teach to the littlest of children—we are recalling the love that exists among Father, Son, and Holy Spirit. This is why love of neighbor is so critical in Christianity: because loving relationship is the very essence of God, and we reflect that essence when we live in loving relationship with others. Think about this carefully. God does not just *have* loving relationships—God *is* loving relationship. And when we participate in such relationships, we participate in God.

By paying attention to your relationships, you are paying attention to the presence of God in your life and in the lives of those you lead and serve.

## Summary: They Held Up His Hands

*Moses' hands grew weary; so they took a stone and put it under him, and he sat on it. Aaron and Hur held up his hands, one on one side, and the other on the other side; so his hands were steady until the sun set.* (Exod. 17:12)

In the story above, as long as Moses kept his arms raised, the Israelites were victorious in battle. When his arms grew weary and he lowered them, however, the Israelites would begin to lose. Thankfully, Aaron and Hur came to the rescue and supported Moses's arms so that Israel would prevail.

In your role as a catechetical leader, you will need others to hold up your weary arms so that you can prevail. Catechetical leaders rely on a network of relationships to sustain them throughout the course of their ministry. These relationships not only support you but also help you to "keep it real." Consider participating in local cluster meetings of catechetical leaders, regional professional organizations of catechetical leaders, and the National Conference for Catechetical Leadership (NCCL), as well as attending catechetical conferences and meeting with a spiritual director.

## For Reflection and Discussion

- What local groups or gatherings of catechetical leaders exist in your area? If you already participate in one, what are the benefits?
- Why might it be good to join a regional professional catechetical organization or a national organization such as the National Conference for Catechetical Leadership? In your view, what is the value of networking with other catechetical leaders?

## Growing as a Catechetical Leader

How are you balancing your responsibilities as a catechetical leader with giving attention to the following: your spouse or significant other, your children, your siblings and other close relatives, your good friends, your mentor, your peers, and your faith community?

Go to www.loyolapress.com/ECL to access the worksheet.

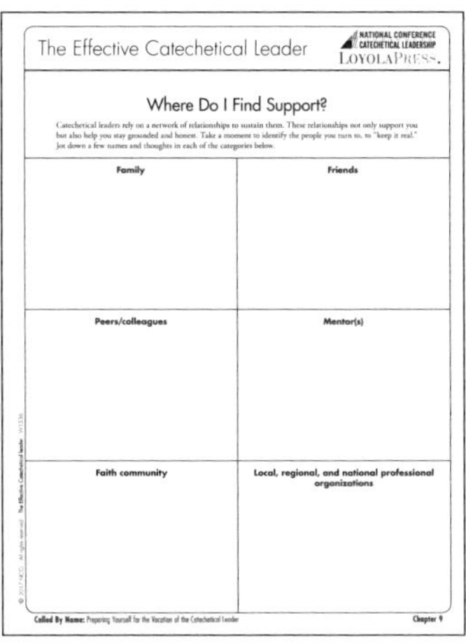

The Effective Catechetical Leader

National Conference Catechetical Leadership

LoyolaPress.

Where Do I Find Support?

Catechetical leaders rely on a network of relationships to sustain them. These relationships not only support you but also help you stay grounded and honest. Take a moment to identify the people you turn to, to "keep it real." Jot down a few names and thoughts in each of the categories below.

| Family | Friends |
| --- | --- |
| **Peers/colleagues** | **Mentor(s)** |
| **Faith community** | **Local, regional, and national professional organizations** |

Called By Name: Preparing Yourself for the Vocation of the Catechetical Leader — Chapter 9

## Suggested Action

Make a list of issues you need help with in your catechetical ministry. Commit to joining a local gathering of catechetical leaders to share your needs and to seek the help and assistance of colleagues as you grow in your ministry.

## For Further Consideration

To further explore the topic of this chapter, consider the following resources:

*The Holy Longing: The Search for a Christian Spirituality.* Richard Rolheiser, O.M.I. (New York: Doubleday, 1999).

*No Man Is an Island.* Thomas Merton (New York: Mariner Books, 1978, first published in 1955).

*Sheltered in the Heart: Spirituality in Deep Friendship.* Gunilla Norris (Pawcatuck, CT: Homebound Publications, 2013).

*Friendship at the Margins: Discovering Mutuality in Service and Mission.* Christopher Heuertz and Christine Pohl (Downers Grove, IL: InterVarsity Press, 2010).

## 10

# How Would Jesus Approach My Role? Leading with Virtue and Humility

When you hear the word *leadership*, a number of thoughts may come to mind, including a montage of historical figures we consider great leaders. Regardless of whether you liked them personally or agreed with their policies, the following people are examples of individuals who exercised great leadership. What do they have in common? Whom would you add to the following list?

- Abraham Lincoln
- Mahatma Gandhi
- Dorothy Day
- Cesar Chavez
- St. Pope John Paul II
- Dr. Martin Luther King Jr.
- St. Mother Teresa of Calcutta
- Harriet Tubman
- Diana, Princess of Wales
- Vince Lombardi
- Sojourner Truth
- Sitting Bull
- Henry Ford
- Alexander the Great
- Margaret Thatcher
- Nelson Mandela

## Take Me to Your Leader

Great leaders have and exercise qualities such as confidence, passion, decisiveness, innovation, persistence, vision, integrity, and the ability to organize, inspire, and empower others. And now the word *leader* is being used to describe *you* as a catechetical minister! What kind of leader will you be? What leadership qualities do you already possess? What leadership qualities do you need to acquire or strengthen?

Book 2 of this Effective Catechetical Leader series—*Pastoral Leadership* by Adrián Alberto Herrera—is fully dedicated to the concept of leadership. Nevertheless, we're going to get a head start on this topic here and now by focusing on the person and leader you are most called to model in your catechetical ministry: Jesus.

## Servant Leadership

If you google "great leaders," many of the 378 million results will identify people from the worlds of politics, sports, and business. While we as catechetical leaders can learn much from these folks, the truth is that we are called to a very different style of leadership because we are called to lead as Jesus led. And if you want to summarize Jesus' leadership style in a nutshell, the place to go is the thirteenth chapter of the Gospel of John:

> Jesus, knowing that the Father had given all things into his hands, and that he had come from God and was going to God, got up from the table, took off his outer robe, and tied a towel around himself. Then he poured water into a basin and began to wash the disciples' feet and to wipe them with the towel that was tied around him. He came to Simon Peter, who said to him, "Lord, are you going to wash my feet?" Jesus answered, "You do not know now what I am doing, but later you will understand." Peter said, "You will never wash my feet." Jesus answered, "Unless I wash you, you have no share with me." Simon Peter said to him, "Lord, not my feet only but also my

> hands and my head!" Jesus said to him, "One who has bathed does not need to wash, except for the feet, but is entirely clean. And you are clean, though not all of you." For he knew who was to betray him; for this reason he said, "Not all of you are clean."

At the core of Jesus' leadership style is the notion of *service*. In his book *Servant Leadership Models for Your Parish*, Dan Ebener talks about Jesus' style of leadership as *servant leadership* (as opposed to what he calls "pedestal leadership"). According to Ebener, servant leadership is focused primarily on addressing the needs and interests of others and advancing a mission far greater than self-interest. In the remainder of this chapter, we'll take a look at how the catechetical leader can answer the call to excellence in three areas of servant leadership—and thus in the area of catechetical leadership.

## Identifying the Gifts of Others

What was the first thing Jesus did when he emerged from the desert after forty days and forty nights? According to the Gospels, he immediately assembled a team. He surrounded himself with people in whom he saw the potential for leadership and service to others. Effective leadership begins not by focusing on oneself, he seems to be saying, but by surrounding oneself with other gifted people.

News flash: The effective catechetical leader is *always* on the prowl for talent! When I was in parish ministry, folks joked that when they saw me walking around with my clipboard, they would run in the opposite direction because "Joe was looking to sign up people for something"! All jokes aside, if you want to be an effective catechetical leader, you must learn to keep your eyes open and spot people whose gifts can be called forth in service of God's kingdom. In fact, it's a key part of your ministry to identify such gifts, affirm them, and call them into action—not for your own benefit but for the spiritual benefit of those you call!

Many people say the reason they never got more deeply involved in parish life or ministry is because no one ever invited them. Here are some practical ways you can become "an inviter" as a catechetical leader.

- Any time you spot a talent or gift—whether in a child, a teen, a young adult, a parent, a middle-aged person, or a senior—acknowledge it out loud and invite the person to use it in service to others. When I learned that one of my catechists' sons played classical guitar, for example, I enlisted him to provide instrumental music for some of our prayer gatherings as well as for Sunday Mass. He joyfully did! And when I discovered that one of my catechists had a passion for social justice and was getting burned out by being a catechist, I invited her to coordinate a "Caring Corner" in the church—a landing spot for donated articles for those in need. She was rejuvenated by her new ministry, and the parish had a new way for people to live out their discipleship.
- By affirming others' gifts and talents, you may be sowing the seeds of future vocations in the catechetical ministry. You don't always have to ask people to "sign up" for duties or "sign on" to particular roles, but if you make an attempt to spot and acknowledge the gifts of others and suggest ways those gifts can be used to serve God's people, you might be surprised by an abundant return.
- By affirming the gifts and talents of others, you are also developing high-quality relationships and assembling a team of "allies"—people who feel compelled to support you because you have taken the time to take notice of them.
- Inviting people is kerygmatic; it is part and parcel of the strategy the apostles used in their first proclamation of the gospel. They invited people into a new way of life that placed Jesus at the

center. For us to be a more evangelizing church, we need to be a more inviting church. We need to invite people to center their lives and talents on Christ. As a catechetical leader, you are perfectly poised to do this.

- Personal invitation is the most effective form of invitation because it springs from, and calls people more deeply into, relationship. You can spend lots of time creating slick Web sites, snazzy bulletin announcements, four-color flyers, and the like (and those are important too!), but the personal invitation—known in some circles as the "friendship factor"—continues to be the single most effective way of recruiting people for anything. The personal touch need not always be face-to-face. A card, a text, an e-mail, a tweet, or a phone call works wonders, too.
- Publicly acknowledging the gifts and talents of others is a powerful tool for the catechetical leader. Take advantage of opportunities to highlight the gifts, talents, achievements, and milestones (for example, birthdays and anniversaries) of children, teens, and adults in your newsletters, bulletin announcements, social-media posts, bulletin boards, and Web sites. The people you acknowledge will be grateful and will look for ways to show it.
- Ritualize people's commitments. Take advantage of opportunities such as Catechetical Sunday (the third Sunday of September) to publicly commission your catechetical staff at Sunday Mass. Consider holding other public rituals such as blessings and commissionings to lift up and make visible the gifts of others—and to send a message loud and clear that these people are living out their baptismal call, just as we are all called to do.
- Finally, one of the most powerful ways to affirm the gifts of others is to privately *and* publicly thank them. Again, the personal touch—a card, a text message, an e-mail, a tweet, or a

phone call—is a most effective thank-you. But don't stop there! Thank people publicly at meetings, appreciation parties/dinners, in newsletters, and on Web sites as well.

## Washing the Feet of Others

Jesus made it very clear that his style of leadership was characterized by serving others. When he got up from the table at the Last Supper and filled a basin with water, wrapped a towel around his waist, and proceeded to wash the feet of his apostles, he was making a profound statement about what it means to be a leader. His apostles (and especially Peter) were thrown for a loop because they were accustomed to "pedestal leadership." As a catechetical leader, one of the most profound ways you can show servant leadership is by confounding those around you who are used to pedestal leadership and engaging in acts of selfless service to those whom you lead.

Let's look at a variety of ways that you, as a catechetical leader, can wash the feet of those you are called to lead.

- **Put the needs of others first.** I am always impressed that when I ask my pastor how he is doing, he often responds by telling me who in the parish is in the hospital or has passed away or is suffering a particular hardship. He doesn't focus on his own needs but on the needs of others—and that is always reflected in his words and actions. At every opportunity, remind yourself to put the needs of others first by encouraging people to share how they are *really* doing when you ask, "How are you?" and by prefacing all of your public remarks with prayer requests for people in need.
- **Lead with humility.** Humility is a virtue that gets a lot of bad press in our contemporary culture because we tend to view it as shaming or belittling oneself. Humility, however, is not about beating ourselves up or even exuding false modesty. Humility is

about seeing ourselves as we really are and, thus, being able to see others and God as they really are too. Humility is not a denial of our self-worth but an affirmation of the inherent worth and dignity of all people and a recognition of our place in that community of people. Humility creates space for others, whereas a bloated sense of self-importance crowds others—and God—out. When we crowd out others and God, we become accustomed to having control—to following our own will. We lose the ability to listen. One of the best ways to practice humility is through mildly self-deprecating humor. People can find it refreshing to learn that you don't take yourself too seriously.

- **Practice speaking of your relationships in egalitarian terms.** I once had a catechetical leader e-mail me through my blog, *Catechist's Journey*, to ask for some help in finding resources for a project she had to tackle very soon. She was apologetic for being so last-minute and felt bad for not following one of my "best practices" of an effective catechetical leader: planning and preparation. I responded by reminding her that "asking your peers for help is considered one of the best practices of catechetical leadership." She thought I meant for her to ask "her peers" instead of bothering me and said that none of her peers was available to help her. I told her that I was affirming her for coming to me for help since I *am* one of her peers! People want to know that you are in the trenches with them, not up in some ivory tower. This is the reason I never introduce myself as Dr. Paprocki; I prefer to be known as Joe.
- **Roll up your sleeves and get your fingernails dirty.** For the catechetical leader, no task is too menial. I often joke with catechetical leaders about putting together the "real" curriculum needed for earning an advanced degree in pastoral ministry: how to make and serve coffee and snacks, how to rearrange furniture

and set up tables and chairs, how to mop up the mess in the restroom, how to clean the crumbs off tables, how to empty out the garbage cans, how to staple packets of handouts, and so on. An effective pastoral minister is never above any of these tasks. To jump in and get to work is what Pope Francis means when he exhorts ministers to "have the smell of the sheep." He wants us to serve the coffee instead of waiting to be served.

- **Be responsive.** Many people will come to you in need of assistance or just in need of some face time. An effective catechetical leader learns how to be immediately responsive to people. Even if you don't have time to solve the issue then and there, it is important to make meaningful eye contact, respond in a genuine way, let others know you have heard them, and promise to follow up—and then do. In this way you build trust and respect and ensure that people will give you the benefit of the doubt down the line. Such responsiveness can also influence not only your peers but also your superiors. It can inspire them to respond to you in the same way you have responded to them and to others. The greater your responsiveness, the greater your sphere of influence, because others perceive you as truly caring instead of as self-interested.
- **Deflect credit.** When people offer you affirmation and gratitude, thank them graciously and then direct attention to all the other people who contributed to whatever success was achieved. The grateful party will take notice and model this variety of humility in the future.
- **Accept blame and admit to mistakes.** Doing this when appropriate—instead of throwing others under the bus—can go a long way in earning the trust of others. Once, during my tenure as a parish pastoral associate and DRE, I worked with a parishioner to plan a simple tuna-casserole meal for parishioners following Good Friday services. We grossly underestimated the

number of people who might show up—and therefore how much tuna casserole to make. We ended up with a big crowd, half of whom went hungry. I got up, took the mike, and took full blame for the mistake, sparing my partner any embarrassment and hoping that he might collaborate with me in the future. It worked—and even those who went hungry felt attended to.

- **Mingle.** I once worked for a boss who would never mingle with the members of his own department. At any meeting or gathering, he would say a few public words and then turn things over to someone else while he hunkered down in a corner and got busy on his phone. This sent a terrible message to the team who looked to him for leadership. One of the most effective ways of solidifying relationships with those you serve is to jump in and mingle with them. This does not mean that you have to become everybody's BFF, but it does mean that you should make a regular effort to show members of your community that you appreciate them, enjoy them, and want to be with them.
- **Ask questions and listen to answers.** Don't do a pretend version of this; do it for real. Share your uncertainties with people you lead, and ask for their insights and opinions. Take time to listen to what people have to say. Let them see you making notes as they respond. Thank them for their feedback and suggestions. And later, let them know how their advice influenced your decisions for the better. This is a great way to show the people you lead that you respect them—but it's also a great way to serve them, because you really do need to know what is on their minds and hearts to respond to their needs.

## Equipping Others

My best friend, who also happens to be named Joe, is a real handyman. I have called on him many a time to take on a home-improvement task that was out of my league. He usually agrees. Inevitably, however, in the middle of the given task, Joe will hand me whatever tool he is using and say, "Okay, your turn." In fact, now that I think about it, one of his handyman projects seems to be *me*! He is always apprenticing me, which is one of the reasons I have always valued his friendship. He has equipped me with many skills that have helped me to grow as a homeowner and, more important, as a person.

As a catechetical leader, you were most likely apprenticed by a mentor in ministry. Now, in turn, one of the most effective leadership strategies you can employ is to equip others with what they need to succeed. You know the old cliché: give someone a fish and he eats for a day, but teach someone to fish and he eats for a lifetime. It's a cliché because it communicates an essential truth. The effective catechetical leader doesn't *distribute* fish but teaches people *how* to fish. Let's take a look at some of the ways you can equip others to succeed in ministry.

- **Share power with others**. Don't be afraid of the word *power*. Scripture tells us that the risen Christ instructed his disciples to remain in Jerusalem until the power (*dunamis* in Greek) of the Holy Spirit came upon them (Acts 1:8). This is God's power, not ours, and it is designed for one purpose only: to achieve God's purpose. Interestingly, God exercises his power through us as leaders in ministry. In other words, God's power is being channeled through *you*. You, in turn, are called to channel that power through others. When we talk about empowering others, we mean that we seek to develop in others the capacity to act on their own. The best way to empower others is to create approaches and techniques that are replicable—that they can easily do on their own. Once, after giving a presentation at a diocesan conference, a high school principal came up to me and asked if I could come to his school to do the same presentation for his faculty. I told him that my schedule would not permit it but that I would give him my PowerPoint presentation—complete with notes and script—and he could do it himself. At first, he thought I was joking and said, "Yeah, right." But when I asked him if he comprehended everything I presented, he said yes. "So there's no reason you can't do this yourself, is there?" I asked, to which he replied, "I guess not!" I have no doubt his presentation was exemplary, because I'm sure he gave it his own twist and flavor under the guidance of the Holy Spirit. God's power is meant to be shared.

- **Build a sense of ownership and commitment.** An effective catechetical leader turns over the reins of various tasks to others—and really, truly lets them have ownership of those tasks. When I was a catechetical leader, one of my catechists was fully certified and was, for all intents and purposes, a master catechist. I asked her if she would become our coordinator for ongoing catechist formation and she happily accepted. From then on, at every catechist meeting, a segment of time was set aside for this catechist to enrich her colleagues. Those segments became known as "Nancy's Part." Her fellow catechists enjoyed learning from one of their peers and were empowered by her example.
- **Give people access to high-quality resources instead of keeping them to yourself.** This impulse is why things go viral on social media: when people find something amazing, they can't wait to share it with others. Doing so reflects well on the sharer and makes him or her look good. As a catechetical leader, one of the ways that you can equip others while polishing your own image is to expose people to amazing resources that can help them develop their skills as catechetical ministers. They'll enrich your parish faith-formation program while they're at it.
- **Attend to the formation of those you lead.** Be sure to use available funds in your budget to invest in the development of those around you. Send people to workshops, seminars, and

conferences, and ask them to share what they learned with the rest of the team when they return. When possible, accompany people to these events to demonstrate your interest in their development and to show that you are personally invested in apprenticing them.

## It Works!

You may never become a famous leader like Gandhi, Harriet Tubman, Lincoln, Dr. King, St. Mother Teresa, or Princess Diana, but as a lay ecclesial minister you are indeed called to lead and inspire others to respond to God's invitation to live as disciples of his Son, Jesus Christ. In the words of author Dan Ebener, "Servant leadership works." May you lead as Jesus led—selflessly serving others, guided by the Holy Spirit, for the glory of God the Father.

## Summary: As I Have Done, So You Must Do

*After [Jesus] had washed their feet, had put on his robe, and had returned to the table, he said to them, "Do you know what I have done to you? You call me Teacher and Lord—and you are right, for that is what I am. So if I, your Lord and Teacher, have washed your feet, you also ought to wash one another's feet. For I have set you an example, that you also should do as I have done to you."* (John 13:12–15)

Leadership begins by focusing not on the head or the heart but on the feet. Washing the feet of others is how Jesus showed us what it meant for him to act as our teacher and Lord. As a catechetical leader, you are called to lead as Jesus leads. We call this "servant leadership" as opposed to the "pedestal leadership" that dominates the secular world. To excel as a servant leader, you need to do three things: identify and affirm the gifts of others, wash their feet (be of humble service to them), and equip them to excel on their own.

## For Reflection and Discussion

- Who is a good servant leader in your life and ministry? What does this leader do, and how does he or she do it?
- What do you need to do in order to be an effective servant leader?

## Growing as a Catechetical Leader

How are you helping others to identify their gifts, and how are you affirming them? How are you washing the feet of those you serve? How are you equipping others to excel on their own so they don't have to rely on your presence?

Go to www.loyolapress.com/ECL to access the worksheet.

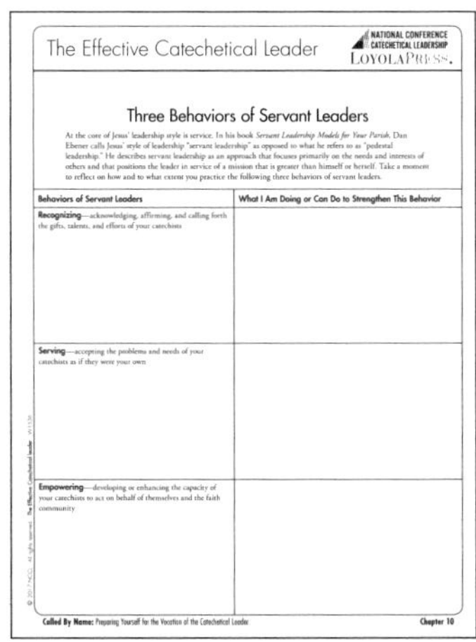
The Effective Catechetical Leader

NATIONAL CONFERENCE CATECHETICAL LEADERSHIP

LOYOLAPRESS.

### Three Behaviors of Servant Leaders

At the core of Jesus' leadership style is service. In his book *Servant Leadership Models for Your Parish*, Dan Ebener calls Jesus' style of leadership "servant leadership" as opposed to what he refers to as "pedestal leadership." He describes servant leadership as an approach that focuses primarily on the needs and interests of others and that positions the leader in service of a mission that is greater than himself or herself. Take a moment to reflect on how and to what extent you practice the following three behaviors of servant leaders.

| Behaviors of Servant Leaders | What I Am Doing or Can Do to Strengthen This Behavior |
|---|---|
| **Recognizing**—acknowledging, affirming, and calling forth the gifts, talents, and efforts of your catechists | |
| **Serving**—accepting the problems and needs of your catechists as if they were your own | |
| **Empowering**—developing or enhancing the capacity of your catechists to act on behalf of themselves and the faith community | |



**Called By Name:** Preparing Yourself for the Vocation of the Catechetical Leader — **Chapter 10**

## Suggested Action

The next time you are with a group of people that you lead, call someone out for a gift or talent they have exhibited; do something that exemplifies humble service to the group (for example, clean up their dishes or tables); and do something to equip someone to excel at a task.

## For Further Consideration

To further explore the topic of this chapter, consider the following resources:

*Servant Leadership Models for Your Parish.* Dan R. Ebener (Mahwah, NJ: Paulist Press, 2010).

*The 7 Habits of Highly Effective People: Powerful Lessons in Personal Change.* Stephen Covey (New York: Simon & Schuster, 1989).

*Leadership Is an Art.* Max DePree (New York: Doubleday, 2004).

# About the Author

**Joe Paprocki**, DMin, is national consultant for faith formation at Loyola Press. He has more than 35 years of experience in ministry and has presented talks and workshops in more than 100 dioceses in North America. He is the author of numerous books, including the best seller *The Catechist's Toolbox*. Joe is a catechist and blogs about his experience at www.catechistsjourney.com.

# The Effective Catechetical Leader Series

Whether you are starting out as a catechetical leader or have been serving as one for many years, **The Effective Catechetical Leader** series will help you use every aspect of this ministry to proclaim the Gospel and invite people to discipleship.

## Called by Name

**Preparing Yourself for the Vocation of Catechetical Leader**

## Catechetical Leadership

**What It Should Look Like, How It Should Work, and Whom It Should Serve**

## Developing Disciples of Christ

**Understanding the Critical Relationship between Catechesis and Evangelization**

## Cultivating Your Catechists

**How to Recruit, Encourage, and Retain Successful Catechists**

## Excellence in Ministry

**Best Practices for Successful Catechetical Leadership**

## All God's People

**Effective Catechesis in a Diverse Church**

Each book in **The Effective Catechetical Leader** series is available for $13.95, or the entire series is available for $65.00.

### To Order:

Call **800.621.1008** or visit **loyolapress.com/ECL**

# The ECL App

## Everything You Need to Be an Effective Catechetical Leader

The ECL app puts wisdom and practical help at your fingertips. Drawn directly from the six books of **The Effective Catechetical Leader** series, ECL provides an opportunity for catechetical leaders to center themselves spiritually each day, focus on specific pastoral issues, and identify go-to strategies for meeting the challenges of serving as an effective catechetical leader.

## Special Features:

- Over 40 unique guided reflections tailored to your individual pastoral ministry needs.
- On-the-go convenience and accessibility on your phone or tablet.
- Modern design, easy-to-use interface, and a source of calm amidst the busy schedule of a catechetical leader.

For more details and to download the app, visit **www.loyolapress.com/ECL**